Turbocharge your ZX

Turbocharge your ZX Spectrum

John Lettice

Longman

ZX SPECTRUM is a Trade Mark of
SINCLAIR RESEARCH LIMITED.

Longman Group Limited
Longman House, Burnt Mill, Harlow,
Essex CM20 2JE, England
and Associated Companies throughout the
world.

© Longman Group Limited 1984

All rights reserved. No part of this
publication may be reproduced, stored in
a retrieval system or transmitted in any
form or by any means, electronic,
mechanical, photocopying, recording or
otherwise, without the prior permission of
the Copyright owner.

First published 1984

ISBN 0 582 91604 6

Printed in UK by Parkway Illustrated Press,
Abingdon

Designed, illustrated and edited by
Contract Books, London

The programs listed in this book have been
carefully tested, but the publishers cannot
be held responsible for problems that
might occur in running them.

Contents

CHAPTER 1
Advanced introduction to the working Spectrum   7

CHAPTER 2
Built-in functions   17

CHAPTER 3
Interactive programming   25

CHAPTER 4
Information handling   31

CHAPTER 5
Handling arrays   41

CHAPTER 6
Introduction to graphics   49

CHAPTER 7
Advanced colour   57

CHAPTER 8
The system variables   67

CHAPTER 9
User-defined graphics   79

CHAPTER 10
Sprites and animation   89

CHAPTER 11
Memory in detail   99

CHAPTER 12
Sound   107

CHAPTER 13
Inferface 1 and interfacing   117

APPENDIX   127

INDEX   155

Note

Many of the programs and routines in this book have been developed, SAVEd and used on Sinclair Microdrives. This means that such programs will need adapting for use on cassette. In general, this is mentioned in the text introducing such programs and routines. However, such programs and routines may easily be identified by a LOAD or SAVE instruction of the following type:

    LOAD * "M";1; "name"
    SAVE * "M";1; "name"

To change these into a form suitable for cassette, use the following:

    LOAD "name"
    SAVE "name"   etc.

However, the order of SAVEing and LOADing data blocks and programs in some of the programs will need to be changed to the order in which they are stored on cassette.

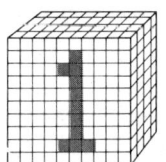

Advanced introduction to the working Spectrum

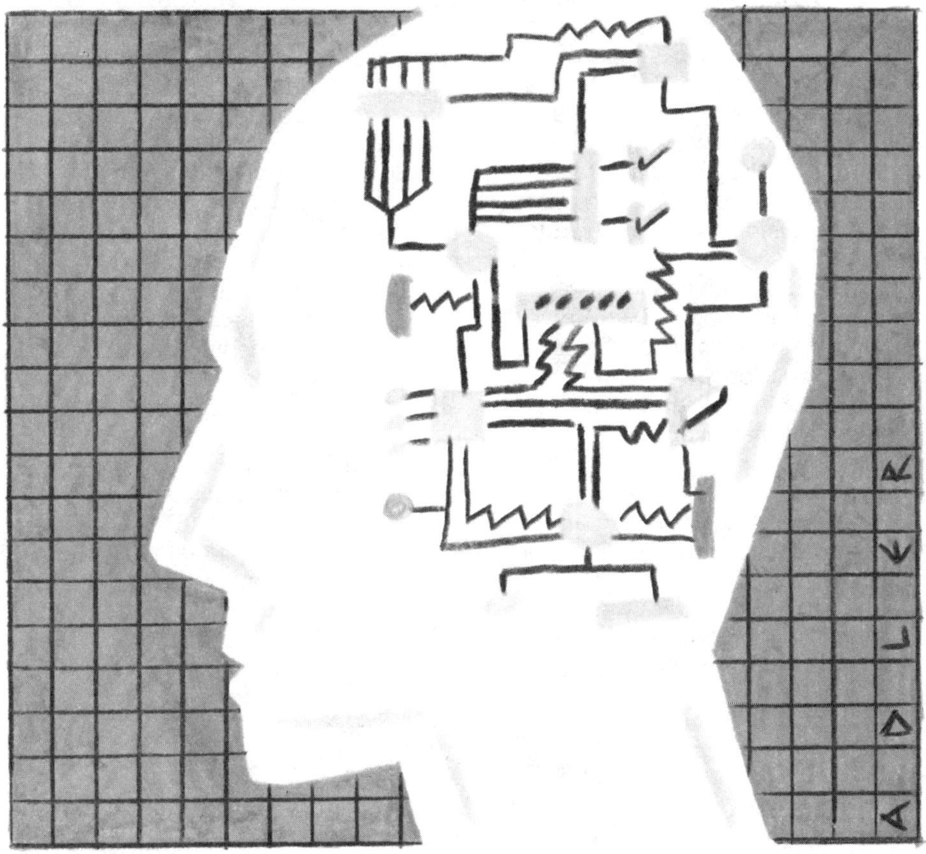

Once you've got to grips with the basics of programming your Spectrum you'll probably be wondering about the direction you should take next. Should you start learning about machine code, should you buy an assembler, or should you try to make your programs more structured?

Of these three courses structure is probably the easiest to learn about, but it's often the hardest to stick to, especially on a machine like the Spectrum, which is much more geared to producing good results than it is to writing elegant programs. But for all that, there are benefits to knowing a little about principles of structure, even if you don't always use them.

Why structure?

So what is structure? As far as effective programming is concerned, structure is about writing your programs in small easily understood sections. Because these can be slotted in and out of the program with the aid of GOSUB your programs can be altered easily, and after you've been writing this way for some time you'll find you have an extensive library of subroutines that you can slot into programs you write in the future.

As your programming improves, and as you add printers, Microdrives and so on, you'll also want to improve or modify your previous efforts, so if you have your programs sectioned off neatly it'll be that much easier to understand what they're doing when you go back to them.

As far as unstructured programming is concerned the main offender is the command GO TO. Let's say you start writing a program, and as you amble through it you suddenly have a brilliant idea about graphics or sound that could be added to the main program.

So you add a GO TO, write the brilliant routine, then add another GO TO putting the program on course. One routine uses two jumps, and what if you have more good ideas of the same sort? Your program soon turns into a spaghetti-like thicket that's hard enough to follow when you've just written it. What happens when you go back to it in a few days (never mind six months) or when you give a copy of the program to one of your friends?

Using subroutines whenever you can stops this happening, and makes everyone's life a lot easier. And think about what you're doing with subroutines. You're breaking a program up into small easily understood sections, and what does this imply? You've got to think about what you're going to do with a program before you start writing it – so structure is as much about planning as it is about using GOSUB.

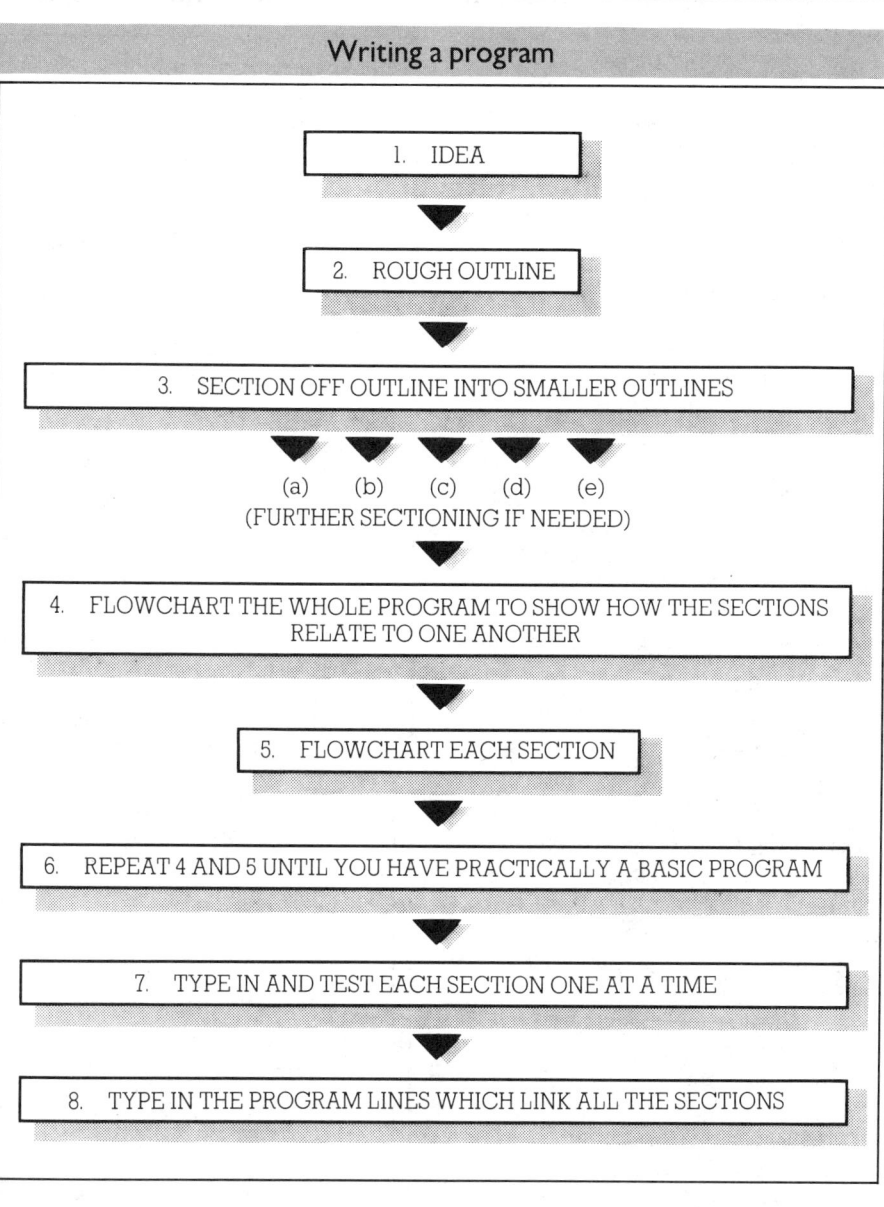

Subroutines

The table here should give you a good idea of how structure and subroutines are linked. Once you've had an idea for a program you can just start hacking it in, but that really is asking for trouble, and you're much better off getting as much of it down on paper as possible before you go anywhere near a computer.

Let's say you decide to write a program involving data handling. As you'll probably be putting data into it in any old order you'll need some form of sort routine to organise it. Once you've written such a routine all you have to do is save it to tape or Microdrive and you can use it in future programs in the form:

```
100  GOSUB 1000:REM SORT
     ROUTINE
999  REM SORT ROUTINE GOES
     HERE
1000 ...
1010 RETURN
```

If you spend a lot of time on little routines like this, maybe in ten years time you'll find you never have to write another one – all you need do is go to your library! Note that putting the REM at 999 instead of 1000 allows you to chop it out to save space later on.

By working out your program structures on paper first you're thinking in terms of programs consisting of control structures. By assuming that the subroutines that actually do the work can be added later you're operating at a much higher level than the Basic language can do, and purists would even say that you should write virtually all the program on paper first.

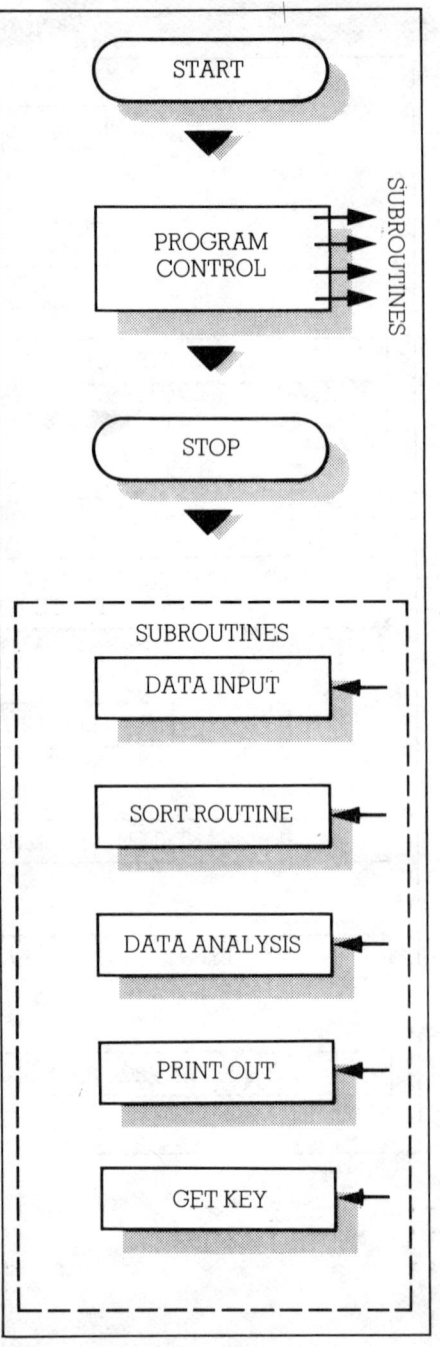

But this is really a hang-over from the days when programmers used mainframes, and computer time was scarce. If you work out the structure on paper, then perfect your subroutines on screen, that will be perfectly adequate. In this case a printer would be useful, as you can't have more than 24 lines of program on the screen at once, and you'll tie yourself in knots handling more than one subroutine in memory at a time, but you can get by without.

AS A RULE

One important thing about subroutines is that they flow evenly and logically – you go into them at the beginning, and come out of them at the end. Look at what's happening here:

```
10  GOSUB 100
20  ...
30  ...
99  REM SUBROUTINE STARTS
100 ...
110 ...
120 IF A$="EXIT" THEN GO TO
    20
130 ...
140 RETURN
```

By writing a program like this you'd be negating the point of subroutines, because you're putting in a jump out of it at line 120. If your subroutine was very long you might want to put in a GO TO to speed the program up (stopping the Spectrum checking through a lot of lines it doesn't need to) but this is a reason for breaking your subroutine up into more, smaller routines, and anyway you can still speed the action by jumping to the RETURN line.

TRY THIS

There's a good reason besides maintaining logical program flow for always exiting a subroutine through the RETURN line. Type in this short program and run it:

```
10  GOSUB 100
20  STOP
100 GO TO 10
```

Now why did that happen? What you've done is exhaust the part of the Spectrum's memory known as the 'stack'. When you say GOSUB 100 in line 10 the computer remembers line 10 in what is effectively a list called the GOSUB stack. The first RETURN it gets to sends it back to 10, so what we've just written is a program that keeps telling the computer to remember one line without telling it it's allowed to forget it.

If you think about it you'll see how the stack operates – if you have nesting subroutines it has to RETURN to the second GOSUB line first before it RETURNs to the first. So the principle is 'last in first out.'

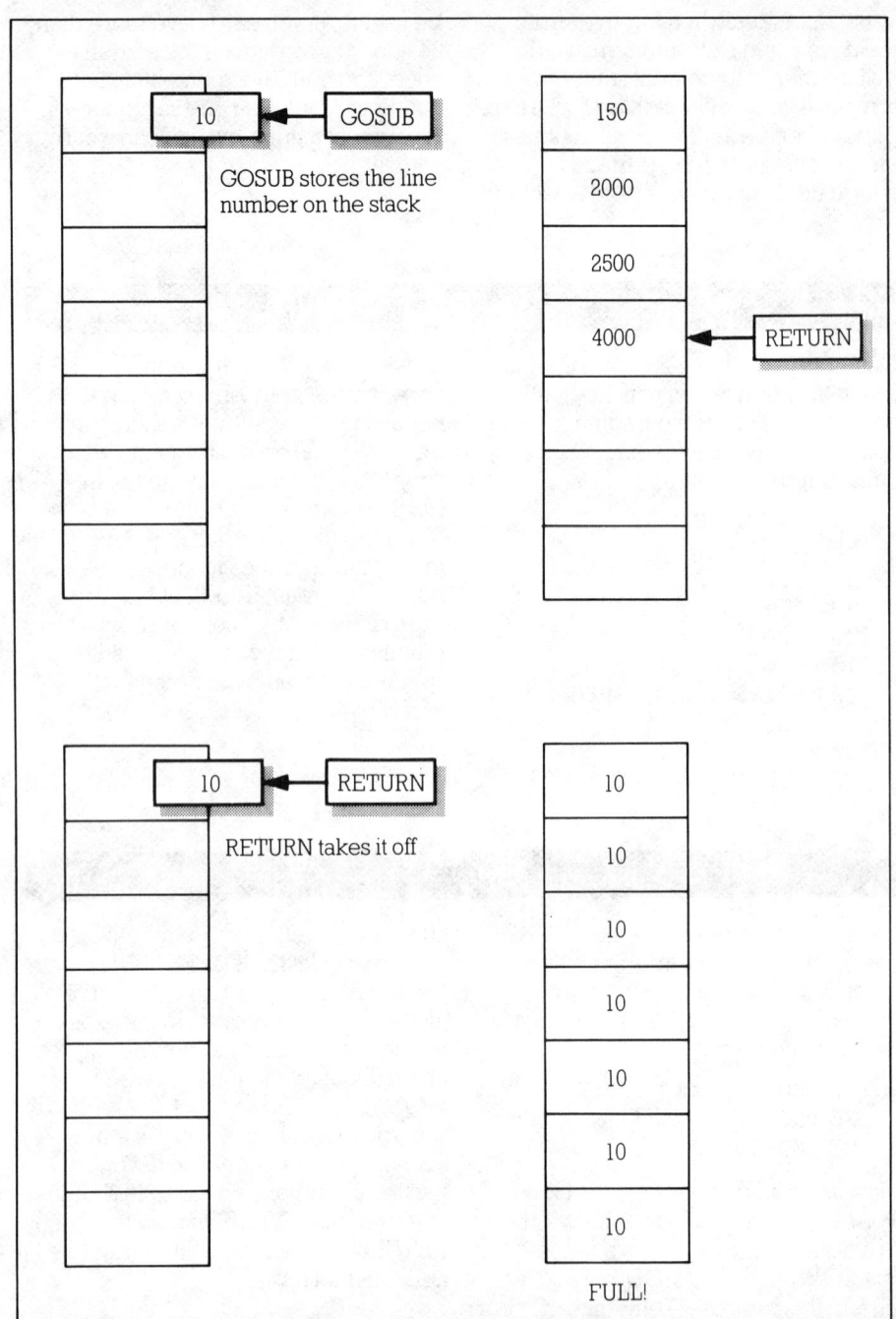

Branches

The next thing you need to consider in program structure is branching, which is basically about how the computer makes decisions. You can think of this quite simply as a way of making the computer check to see if something is true, and if it is, taking a specified action. This generally takes the form IF *condition* THEN *action*.

Along with IF...THEN you use the symbols =, <, > and < >, which are known as logical operators, and mean

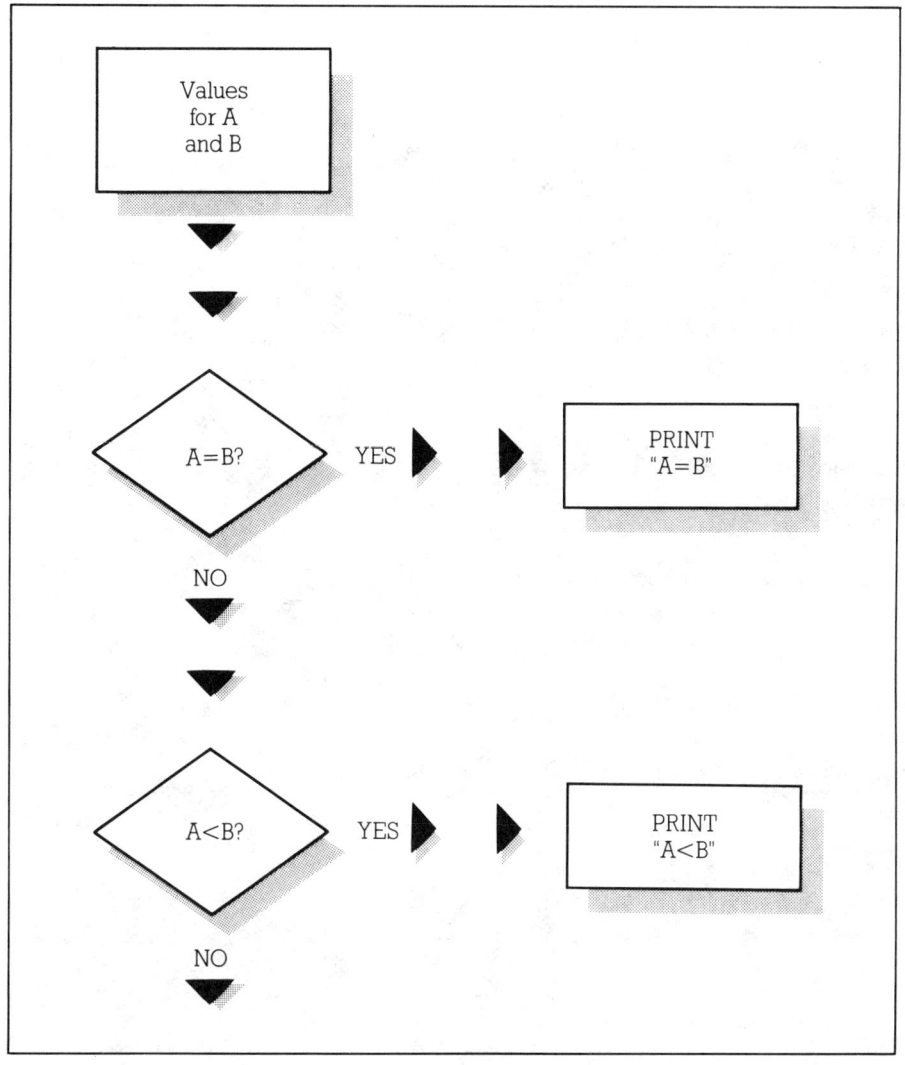

equal to, less than, greater than and not equal to respectively. AND, OR and NOT are also operators.

```
10  LET A=10: LET B=5
20  IF A=B THEN PRINT "A=B"
30  IF A<B THEN PRINT "A IS
    LESS THAN B"
40  IF A>B THEN PRINT "A IS
    GREATER THAN B"
50  IF A<>B THEN PRINT "A
    DOES NOT EQUAL B"
```

You can also combine conditions using the operators AND and OR:

```
60  IF A=10 OR B=10 THEN
    PRINT "ONE CONDITION IS
    TRUE"
70  IF A=10 AND A=B THEN
    PRINT "BOTH CONDITIONS
    ARE TRUE"
```

Other Basics

Spectrum Basic lacks a number of structures that are designed to make organised programming easier. For example, some micros allow you to use lines like this:

```
100 ON X GOSUB
    200,300,400,500,600
```

This is a handy formulation allowing you to specify different subroutines depending on the value of X. If X=1 than the micro GOSUBs 200, if X=2 it GOSUBs 300 and so on. But you won't get very far if you try this with the Spectrum!

The easiest way to get round this is to use IF X=1 THEN GOSUB 200, etc, but there is a way of simulating the structure:

```
100 GOSUB (100 AND X=1)
    +(200 AND X=2) +(300
    AND X=3) . . .
```

What you're doing here is using the Spectrum's ability to distinguish between true and false. If you say 'X=1' and X does not equal 1, then the Spectrum thinks '0' or false. If it thinks '1' then X *does* equal 1. Now by saying (100 AND X=1) you are specifying that the second condition needs to be true before it does GOSUB 100. Note that (100+(X=1)) means something completely different.

A less useful construct not present in Spectrum Basic is IF...THEN...ELSE. This is used like this:

```
10  IF A=B THEN PRINT "A
    IS EQUAL TO B" ELSE
    PRINT "A DOES NOT
    EQUAL B"
```

You'd duplicate this less elegantly by saying:

```
10  IF A=B THEN PRINT "A
    IS EQUAL TO B":GO TO
    30
20  PRINT "A DOES NOT
    EQUAL B"
30  .....continue program
```

But again you can use true/false:

```
10  PRINT ("A IS EQUAL TO
    B" AND A=B)+("A DOES
    NOT EQUAL B" AND
    A<>B)
```

Loops

The final design structure we'll be dealing with in this chapter is the FOR...NEXT loop, which helps you avoid having to type in repetitive lines. Think of this:

```
10  FOR I=1 TO 20
20  BEEP 1,I
30  NEXT I
```

Here you're using a simple FOR...NEXT loop to do something that would otherwise take you 20 lines.

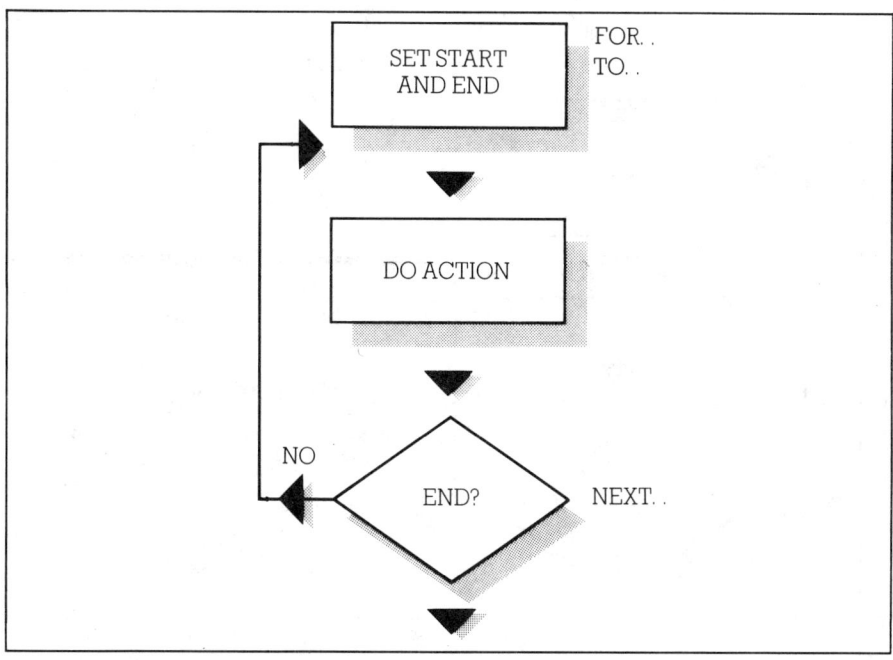

TRY THIS

It's quite easy, and useful, to produce nesting FOR...NEXT loops, or loops inside one another:

```
10  FOR I=1 TO 12
20  PRINT "Table for ";I
30  FOR J=1 TO 12
40  PRINT I;"x";J;"=";I*J
50  NEXT J
60  NEXT I
```

This will print out the multiplication tables up to 12×12. Note that you have to finish the last loop first (the J loop in this case) otherwise you'll confuse yourself. Try swopping round lines 50 and 60 to see what happens.

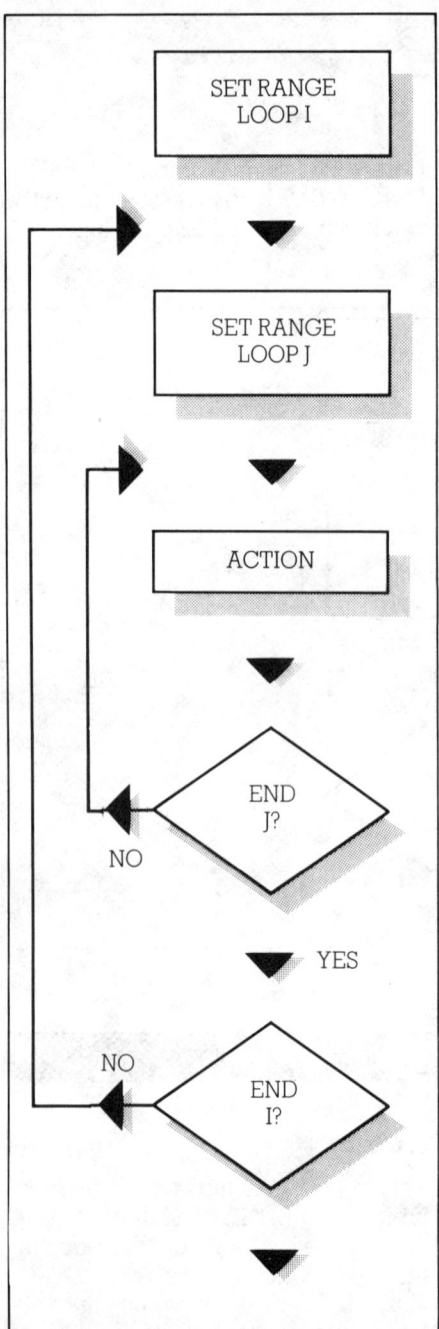

AS A RULE

Just as with GOSUBs you shouldn't jump out of a FOR...NEXT loop before it's finished. For example:

```
10  FOR I=1 TO 50
20  IF I=25 THEN GO TO 40
30  NEXT I
40  ....continue program
```

You'll have just the same sort of problems here as you would jumping out of a subroutine, so you should use IF I=25 THEN LET I=51:GO TO 30 to take you to the end of it.

━━━━━ Checklist ━━━━━

In this chapter you've learned:

☐ Why you should try to write structured programs.

☐ How and why to use subroutines (and how not to use them).

☐ How to use branches, and how to simulate the features of more structured Basics in Spectrum Basic.

☐ How to use IF...THEN.

☐ How and why to use loops for repetitive tasks.

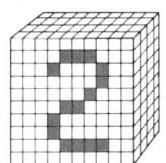

Built-in functions

All computers spend their time calculating with numbers and most programs need to be able to manipulate numbers in various ways. These methods of manipulation fall into two main categories, functions and operators. Operators are such things as + − */ and need a number either side of them, ie PRINT 2+2.

Functions, on the other hand, take a number as their argument and do something to it, such as SIN which converts its argument into a sine. They always produce a result, so when using them you must always make sure that the result is used, ie:

```
LET A=INT(10.2)
PRINT SIN(PI)
```

RND

The RND function is one of the most useful built-in functions on the computer, although it is not strictly a function since it does not work directly on an argument. It can be used for a number of things, from selecting random answers to a question like this:

```
10 INPUT"How are you
   feeling today";A$
15 PRINT"That's good 'cause
   I feel ";
20 LET B=INT(RND*4)+1
25 GOSUB (40 AND B=1)+(50
   AND B=2)+(60 AND
   B=3)+(70 AND B=4)
30 STOP
40 PRINT"Great.":RETURN
50 PRINT"Fine.":RETURN
60 PRINT"OK.":RETURN
70 PRINT"Ugh!":RETURN
```

Or, even simpler, you can print stars onto the screen with this:

```
10 FOR T=0 TO 100
20 PLOT INT(RND*255)+1,INT
   (RND*176)+1
30 NEXT T
```

Normally you will want the result of a call to RND to be a whole number (integer) and as above, the form:

```
INT(RND*R)+1
```

can be used, where R is the range from 1 to R. This can be a little tedious to type in if there are a lot of RND selections to be made. A neater alternative is to define a function to produce the desired result, ie:

```
DEF FN R(R)=INT(RND*R)+1
```

Once defined within a program, this can be used to produce integer random numbers as follows:

```
PRINT FN R(6)
```

giving a number from 1 to 6 at random, the throw of a dice for example, or LET CARD=FN R(13).

A thing to note about RND is that it isn't truly random since the computer switches on with everything set to a predefined value. Switching off and on and printing RND gives the same number every time.

RND produces what is known as a pseudo random number which is created by taking a seed number and performing a series of operations on it with a set formula producing another number. This result is then given as the result of RND; it is also made the new seed with which the next random number is produced. This can be demonstrated with the following program which produces pseudo random numbers between 0 and 6. from a simple formula:

```
10 INPUT"Seed=";A
20 LET A=(A*75)+19200
40 LET A=A-INT
   (A/256)-INT(A/256)
45 LET A=A-(INT
   (A/65536)*65536)
50 PRINT INT(A/10000)
60 GOTO 20
```

The RND function within the Spectrum is a lot more efficient and complex than this and hence produces a longer series. It will, however, eventually repeat itself.

The seed can be set on the Spectrum with RANDOMIZE and if you try:

```
10 RANDOMIZE 1
20 PRINT RND
30 RANDOMIZE 1
40 PRINT RND
```

you'll see that the randomize statement causes the RND function to start at a specific place in the series of random numbers. This can be both an advantage and a disadvantage depending on the stage of program development. If you are testing a program that uses random numbers it is useful to have RND start at the same place so that the results can be verified. However, once the program works, having RND start in the same place every time causes the program to be predictable in which case there is no point in using RND at all. The way out of this is to reset RANDOMIZE at the begining of the program. This is actually easier than it sounds since there are a number of locations within the Spectrum that change too quickly to be predicted and hence are effectively random. One of these is 23672, the number of TV frames, which changes every 20 mS. If the first line of the program includes RANDOMIZE PEEK 23672 the chances of it picking the same number every time the program is run is 1 in 256, a lot more random than many other methods.

INT

In the section on RND we used INT to get whole numbers from decimals with:

```
PRINT INT(RND*10)+1
```

The INT function is used to change the format of the number and split it into two halves, each side of the decimal point, and then feed back the left hand side as the result, ie INTeger it, so:

```
PRINT INT(123.456)
```

prints 123. One thing to note about this function is that it rounds the number down so INT(23.999) gives 23 and not 24 as one might expect. It may be necessary to round the number in the accepted way, ie round the decimal part up if it is .5 or more and round down .499999 and less. This is easily done by adding 0.5 to the number before INTing it. Try this:

```
10 INPUT"Price=";A
20 PRINT"Rounds to:";
   INT(A+.5)
30 GO TO 10
```

This is quite useful when dealing with financial amounts since 55.55 pence is normally taken to be 56 pence.

ABS and SGN

Another function that changes the format of a number is ABS. This is used to strip off the sign from the front of the number and make it positive no matter what it was before. So ABS(−2) will give 2 and so will ABS(2). This function is useful for a number of things, such as making sure that when printing or plotting onto the screen, no values are allowed that go negative and hence give an error. Even more useful is making a toggle allowing one key to be used to turn something on or off. Like this:

```
10 LET T=1
20 IF T=1 THEN PRINT "PUSH
   OFF"
30 IF T=0 THEN PRINT "PUSH
   ON"
40 LET A$=INKEY$:IF A$=""
   THEN GO TO 40
45 PAUSE 0
50 LET T=ABS(T-1)
60 GOTO 20
```

A function very close to ABS is SGN. This returns plus one for any positive number and minus one for negative numbers. The odd one out is zero for which SGN gives 0 since it is debatable whether 0 is positive or negative. As a demonstration try:

```
10 INPUT A
20 PRINT A;" is ";
30 IF SGN(A)=-1 THEN PRINT
   "negative.":GO TO 60
40 IF SGN(A)=1 THEN PRINT
   "positive.":GO TO 60
50 PRINT "zero."
60 GOTO 10
```

A much neater way of doing this is to replace lines 30, 40 and 50 with one line:
```
PRINT ("negative." AND
SGN(A)=-1) ("positive." AND
SGN(A)=1); ("zero." AND
SGN(A)=0)
```

SIN, COS, TAN, ASN, ACS, ATN

These are the trigonometric functions and are used for messing around with angles. They fall into two sections since ASN does the opposite of SIN, ie:

```
10 LET A=SIN(2.5)
20 LET B=ASN(A)
30 PRINT A;" is the SIN of ";B
```

so

```
ASN is antiSIN or arc SIN
ACS is antiCOS or arc COS
ATN is antiTAN or arc TAN
```

Most people are used to working with angles between 0 and 360 degrees, but the Spectrum (and most other computers) uses the mathematician's form of splitting a circle into 2*PI radians.

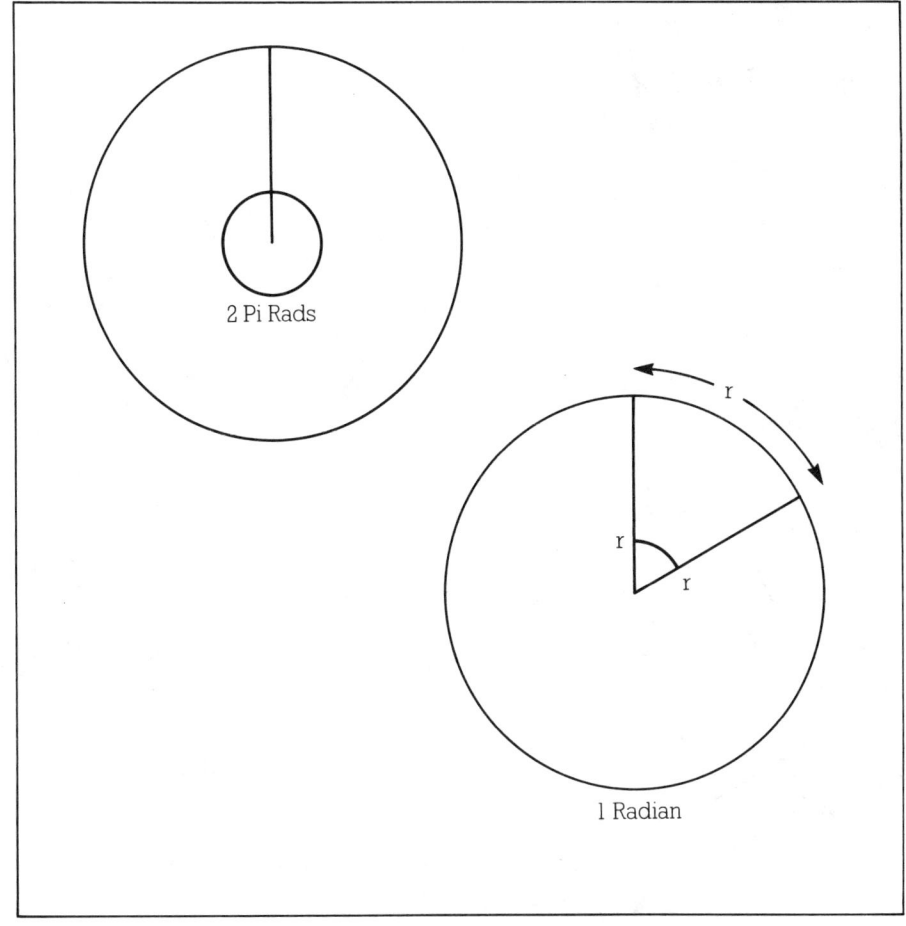

2 Pi Rads

1 Radian

Built-in functions

> **Conversion of degrees to radians and back**
>
> Since 2*PI radians =360 degrees, to convert degrees, to radians just multiply PI/180 or define the function:
>
> DEF FN r(A)=A*PI/180
>
> **To go the other way multiply by 180/PI or use the function:**
>
> DEF FN d(A)=A*180/PI

The Spectrum is better at this than many computers as it includes PI as a predefined number and so conversions can be handled a lot more easily.

SIN, COS and TAN are defined using a right-angle triangle and are useful for graphics handling. For instance, suppose you draw a square on the screen with:

```
 10  LET X=20:LET Y=20
100  PLOT X,Y
110  DRAW 20,0
```

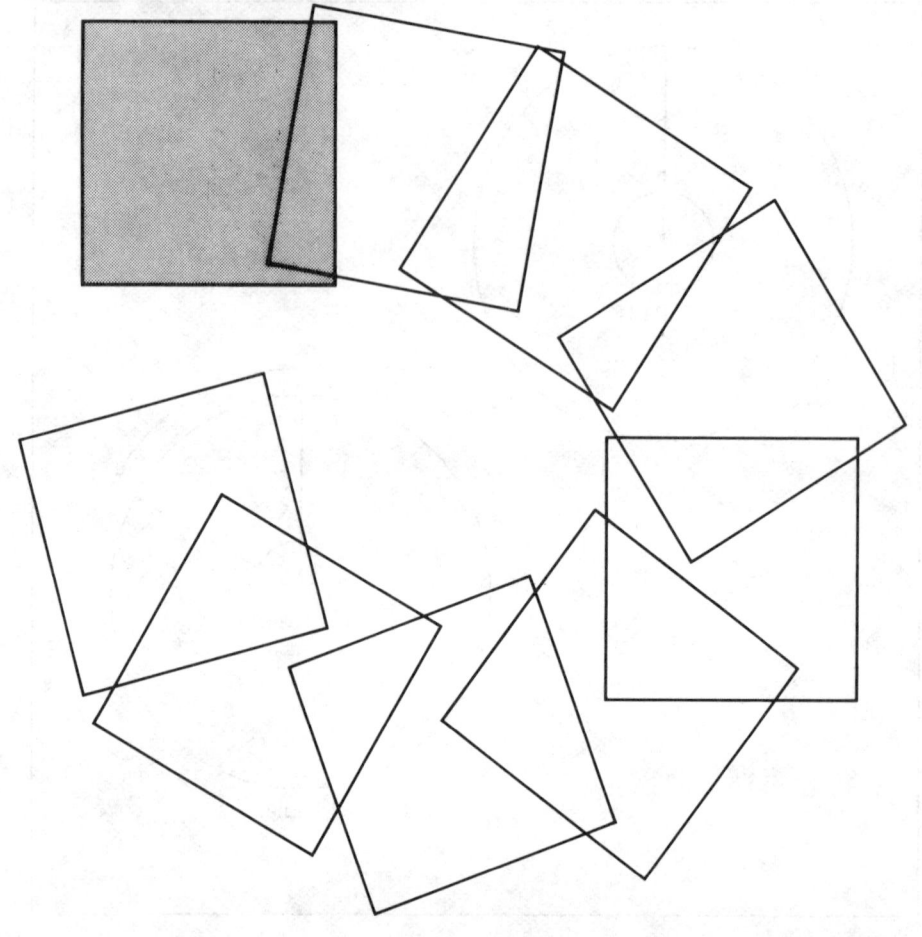

```
120 DRAW 0,-20
130 DRAW -20,0
140 DRAW 0,20
```
and you want to turn it through 45 degrees to get a diamond. SIN and COS can be used to calculate the new positions for the lines. Alter the square program to this:
```
10  LET X=40:LET Y=40
15  INPUT "Angle=";A
16  LET A=FN r(A)
20  GOSUB 100:REM DRAW
    SQUARE
30  STOP
40  DEF FN r(A)=A*PI/180
100 PLOT X,Y
110 DRAW 20*SIN(A),
    20*COS(A)
120 DRAW 20*SIN(A+(PI/2)),
    20*COS(A+(PI/2))
130 DRAW 20*SIN(A+PI),
    20*COS(A+PI)
140 DRAW 20*SIN(A+(3*PI/
    2)),
    20*COS(A+(3*PI/2))
150 RETURN
```
Adding and altering the following lines will give a nice pattern.
```
15 FOR T=0 TO 360 STEP 10
16 LET A=FN r(T)
25 NEXT T
30 STOP
```
The results of all these functions can be nicely illustrated using graphs of which SIN is the easiest. Try this:
```
10 FOR T=0 TO 2*PI STEP
   0.1
20 PLOT T*10,SIN(T)*10+50
30 NEXT T
```
This displays the shape of a sine wave and if you replace SIN by COS or even RND you will get a better idea of what these functions do. The following program can be used to display the various functions, and even mixtures of them, such as SIN(1−SIN(3*T)).
```
5   GOSUB 100 : REM DRAW
    AXES
10  INPUT"Enter function:";
    A$
20  FOR T=0 TO 2*PI
    STEP .1
30  PLOT T*23,VAL(A$)*
    50+50
40  NEXT T
50  GOTO 10
99  REM DRAW AXES
100 PLOT 0,0
110 DRAW 0,100
120 PLOT 0,50
130 DRAW 150,0
140 RETURN
```
Note that when entering functions you should use the single key entry system.

━━━━━━━━━━━ Checklist ━━━━━━━━━━━

In this chapter you've learned:

☐ How RND works and how to define a user function to give a specific range of values.

☐ How the INT function works and when to use it.

☐ How ABS and SGN work and what they are useful for.

☐ How SIN, COS, TAN, ASN, ACS and ATN work and how they are useful for graphics.

☐ How to set up some user-defined functions to convert degrees to radians and radians to degrees.

Projects

☐ Use the last graph plotting program with a mixture of functions including such things as ABS and SGN to see how they work. See if you can improve the axes by labelling them.

☐ Try writing your own pseudo random number generator that can generate a long sequence of random numbers.

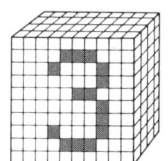

Interactive programming

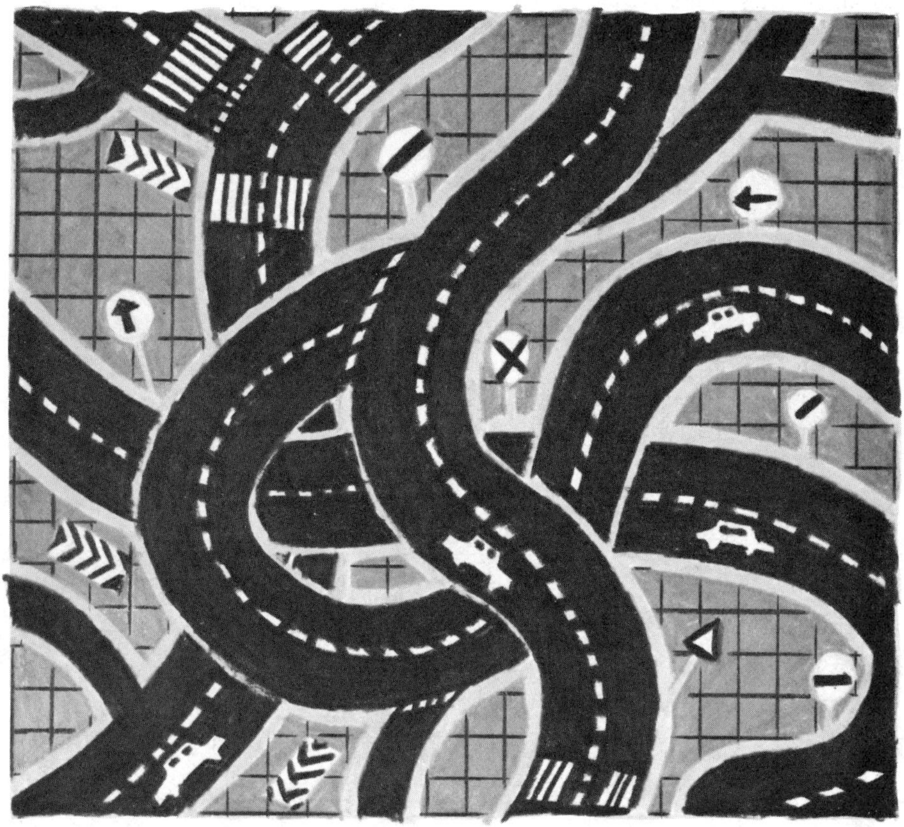

When we say 'interactive programming' we mean something quite simple – how you and your Spectrum act together. You could design a program that was hardly interactive at all, for example a graphics demonstration program that simply cycled through a series of pictures without you having to do anything, but in most cases you will physically have to press keys and give the computer some information at various points in the program.

So 'interactive programming' deals with how you give information to the computer, and how the computer gives you its information back, on the screen or on a printer. Naturally, if you want your programs to be as useful as possible, you will also want to be able to present the computer's information in as clear a way as possible, and you'll want the information you give the computer to be easy to type in, and difficult for either you or the Spectrum to make a mess of. This chapter is intended to help you do this.

Why do you do this? Naturally *you're* not an idiot, but as one day you may want to sell your programs, you'll want to make them as idiot-proof as possible! For example, let's say you use the following lines:

```
10  INPUT "Enter a number ";A
20  GO TO 10
```

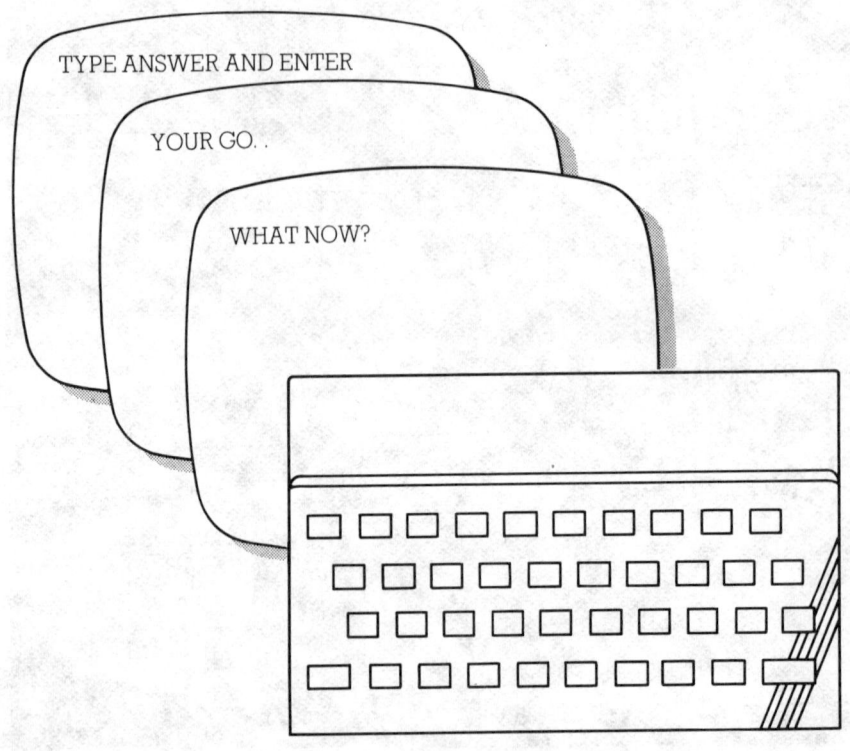

You've told the user to type in a number, so if you type 1,2,3 and so on that's fine. But what you think is a number and what the computer thinks is a number may be two separate things. Type 'one' Enter, and you'll see one case of the computer misunderstanding you. And remember that while you think 1,000 is a number, the one the computer expects is 1000. In this case we've only messed up a two line program, but imagine that those two lines are part of an address book program, that you've just typed in 100 addresses, and then you absent-mindedly press the wrong key – nasty thought, isn't it?

Getting information

The Spectrum has two main ways of getting information from the user, INPUT and INKEY$. Some other computers have a command GET, or GET$, which is used in the form GET A or GET A$, and this tells the computer to wait for the user to press a key. It is similar to INKEY$, but INKEY$ doesn't wait for a key to be pressed, so you're at a disadvantage.

Or are you? You can simulate it like this:

```
10 IF INKEY$="" THEN GO TO 10
```

The Spectrum will now wait at this line until you press a key, and when you do this it will skip to the next line.

But what about our little INPUT problem? First ask yourself what's making the Spectrum return an error when you type in 'one'. What you're doing is typing in a string when it expects a number, whereupon it tells you where to get off. So you need to prepare for the worst possible case, and this means writing the program so that it will handle strings without stopping.

Try this:

```
10 INPUT "Enter a number from 0-9";A$
20 IF CODE A$<48 OR CODE A$>57 THEN BEEP .5,1: GO TO 10
30 LET A=VAL A$
```

What this little program does is accept whatever string the user types in, checks its CODE value, then only goes on to line 30 if this value is between 48 and 57. The CODEs from 48 to 57 are of course the CODEs of the numbers 0–9.

Now you could try this for larger numbers, but the problem is that CODE only returns the value of the first character of a string. So if you typed in something like 2c32 it would read the CODE of 2 only, and you'd still be messed up. But never fear, all you've got to do is get the Spectrum to check the characters in A$ individually.

One way of doing this is to loop through the characters one at a time:

```
20 FOR N=1 TO LEN A$
30 IF CODE A$(N TO N)<48 OR CODE A$(N TO N)>57 THEN BEEP .5,1: GO TO 10
```

27
Interactive programming

```
40  NEXT N
50  LET A=VAL A$
```

You now have a routine that checks everything you type in letter, or rather *character* by character, and gives a petulant BEEP if you've made a mistake. The expression A$(N TO N) is the Spectrum's long-winded way of specifying an individual character in a string, so if N is 5 you're actually saying A$(5 TO 5), which specifies the fifth character in the string. A$(5 TO 6) specifies the fifth and sixth, and so on.

You could start off with DIM A$(X), which would have the added advantage of allowing you to control the size of the number (or what will eventually become a number) by limiting it to whatever you choose as X. You could make your program even more bomb-proof in this case by also trapping errors by comparing the length of the string typed in with N, and if it was too great, again going back to line 10.

What you're doing here is thinking of ways to trap errors. Obviously you can't trap them all when you're writing the program, but if you think about what you're doing, and update your programs when you run into another problem, you'll eventually have a much more professional finished product.

A rule

When you're writing a program try not to mix INPUT and INKEY$ too much. Obviously if the program is asking for a number or a filename (both greater than one character) then INPUT is useful, but in the main using a mixture of the two is confusing, as the user will tend to press Enter while the program's executing.

TRY THIS

It's possible to trap errors in inputs by making any number of characters you like illegal. To do this, you should look up the character codes in Appendix A of the Spectrum manual. All you have to do then is to trap any characters with codes outside your chosen range:

```
1000  PAUSE 0
1010  IF INKEY$=CHR$(13) OR
      INKEY$=CHR$(32) THEN
      GO TO 1030
1020  IF CODE(INKEY$)<65 OR
      (CODE(INKEY$)>90 AND
      CODE(INKEY$)<97) OR
      CODE(INKEY$)>122 THEN
      GO TO 1000
1030  PRINT INKEY$;
1040  GO TO 1000
```

If you RUN this program you'll see that it operates like a typewriter. You've made all characters except for letters of the alphabet (upper and lower case) illegal. Not much of a typewriter though, is it, because you can't use any punctuation.

Check up the codes in the manual and you'll find CHR$(13) is Enter (new line) and CHR$(32) is Space. So in line 1010 you're checking to see if the key pressed is one of these two, and if so skipping the next line, which would otherwise rule them illegal. Delete line 1010 to see this.

Other points of interest are the PAUSE statement in line 1000, which we're using to stop the keys we press being repeated, and the semicolon in line 1030, which makes sure the next character is printed adjacent to the last.

Checklist

In this chapter you should have learned:

- [ ] What interactive programming means.
- [ ] The differences between INPUT and INKEY$.
- [ ] How to use CODE to check that the user of a program is hitting the right keys, thus avoiding errors.

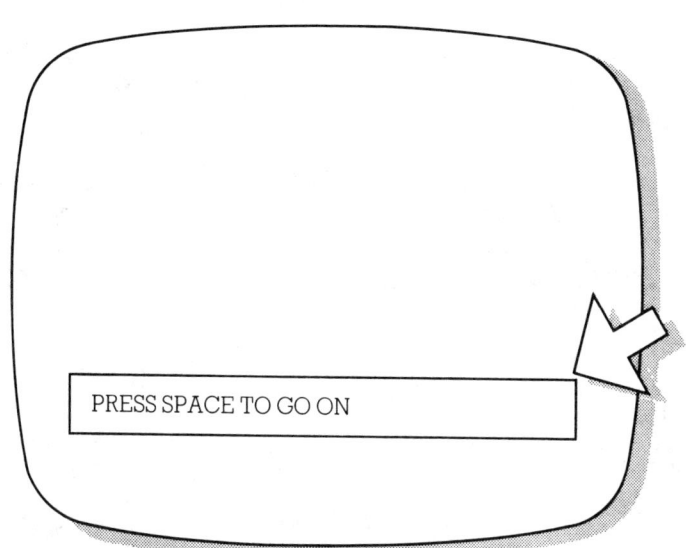

Projects

- Write a short routine that allows you to INPUT names and addresses, excluding numeric input for the first row (where the name should go). You could also insist on the first part of the next row being a number, but you'd have to allow for a symbol in case the house didn't have a number, say '#'. Keep tidying this one up until it's bomb-proof.

- Rewrite our poor man's word processor so that it will also accept punctuation and numbers.

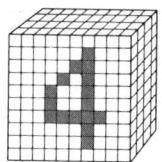

Information handling

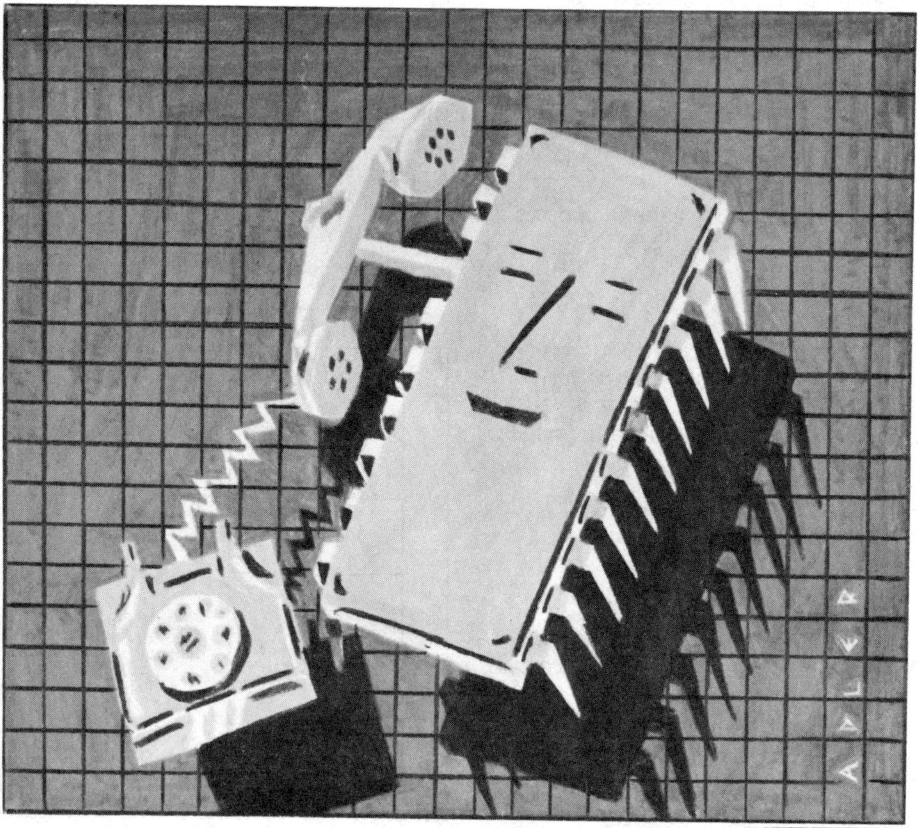

Information handling may not sound very exciting, but if you think about it you'll find it's crucial to you being able to write programs that *are* exciting on your Spectrum. After all, what does a computer do? It stores information in the form of numbers, so that when you tell it to do something it consults the information it's storing and acts accordingly.

And it doesn't matter whether the information you're dealing with is a space invader or the size of your bank balance – as far as the Spectrum is concerned it's all the same. What *does* matter is how efficient the way you tell the Spectrum to deal with that information is.

Note pads

Computers using the Basic language have several forms of information storage available to them, the most obvious being in the form of DATA statements. A DATA statement is essentially just a list of numbers or letters that you tuck at the end of a program:

```
10 FOR A=1 TO 10
20 READ B
30 PRINT A;" times two is ";B
40 NEXT A
50 DATA 2,4,6,8,10,12,14,
   16,18,20
```

Now this may look like a silly program to you, particularly as you know the two times table, and you also know that:

```
10 FOR A=1 TO 10
20 PRINT A;" times two is ";A*2
30 NEXT A
```

is shorter and does exactly the same thing. But think about it – as we've said, you already know the two times table, so why go to the trouble of working it out over and over again? DATA statements, you see, are lists of information that you already have, and there are times when it's a lot faster for a program to just look up the list rather than reinvent the wheel over and over again.

What is happening in our DATA statement version of the program is that line 10 is counting through ten different values for A, and for each different value it reads B once. By READ B we mean go down to the Ath (i.e. first, second, third etc) DATA statement you find and set a new value

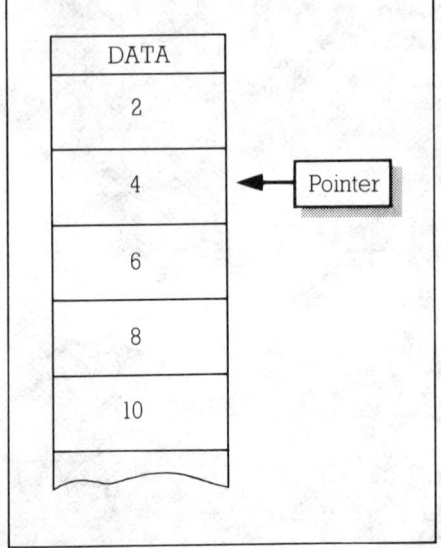

for B each time. It's then just a matter of the program doing what you've told it to do with B.

One thing to remember about DATA statements is that you can only READ them once unless you use the RESTORE command. In the case above you'd say RESTORE 50 (*ie* reactivate the DATA in line 50) and then you could READ it for a second time, from another line if you wished. What you're doing with RESTORE is resetting something called the DATA pointer, which is used to keep track of where you are in the DATA statement, and stores the value of the last piece of DATA you READ. You can have as much or as little DATA in a line as you wish – try changing it to:

```
50  DATA 2,4,6,8,10
60  DATA 12,14,16,18,20
```

and you'll find it doesn't make a scrap of difference.

We know that READ and DATA are useful for storing information we already know, such as user-defined graphics or the notes for tunes, but what if we want to store information that varies? In that case we have to look elsewhere.

Ways with arrays

We've looked at the note pad, and seen its limitations, but fortunately the Spectrum also has a filing cabinet available! The easiest way to think of an array is as a grid of boxes, or a table, where you decide how many boxes are in the grid.

You set these boxes with the DIM command, and if you look at the illustration below you'll see how it's

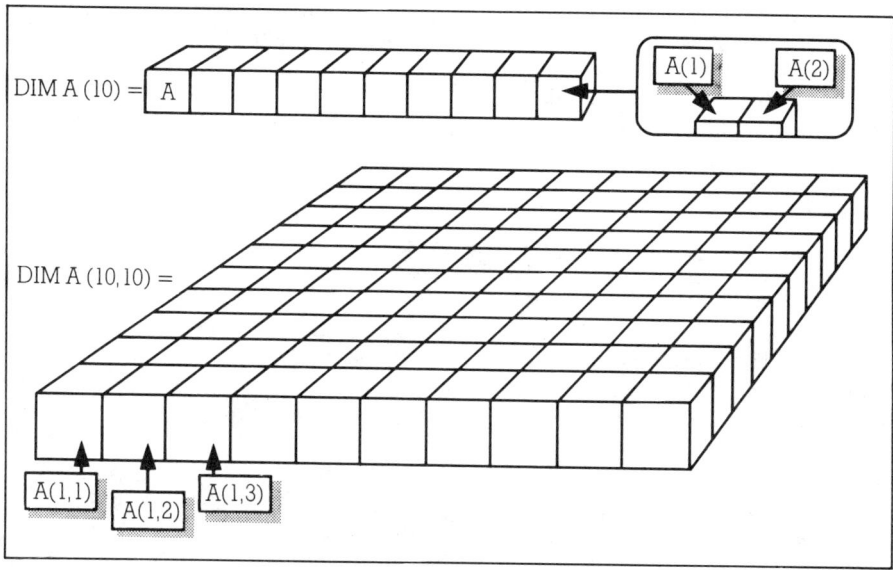

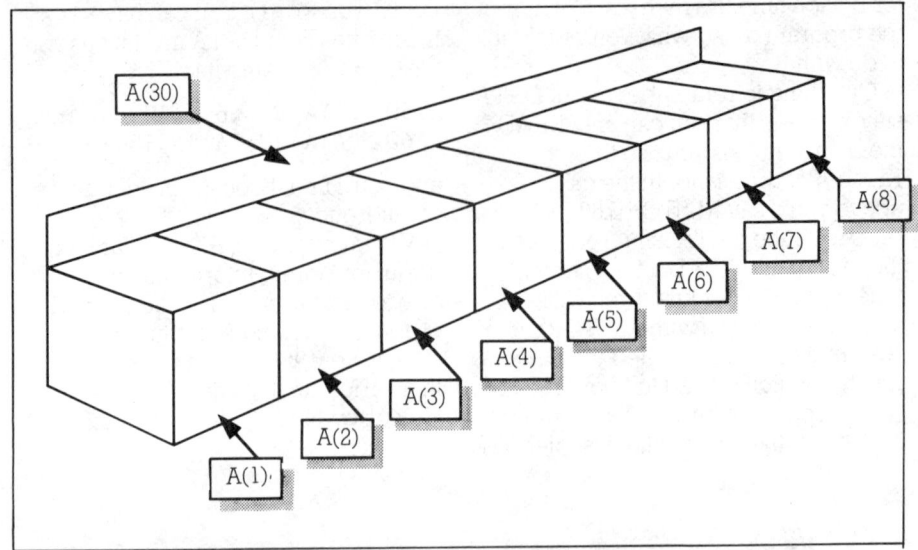

done. By saying DIM A(10) you're setting up storage space for ten pieces of information which you can refer to as A(1) to A(10). By saying DIM A(10,10) you're setting up space for 10×10, ie *100* pieces of information from A(1,1) to A(10,10). You can imagine an array 10×10×10, which would be DIM A(10,10,10), and you can produce four or more dimensioned arrays – the only limit is the amount of memory in the Spectrum.

Think of it like this – DIM A(30) instructs the Spectrum to set up a large box containing 30 smaller boxes called A(0), A(1), A(2) and so on. These smaller boxes are called subscripts – this should give you an idea of what the Spectrum means when it gives you an error message that says 'subscript wrong'.

Organisation

So far we've only dealt with arrays holding numbers, ie *numeric* arrays, but you can store string data in arrays (including user-defined graphics) in *string* arrays. These differ simply by being DIMensioned DIM A$(X).

Suppose you want to keep a record of a set of information, such as addresses, or details about your record collection. The information can be broken down into a number of different sections that you can deal with easily, and each of which stores a different piece of information. These sections are called fields, and the collection of fields on one subject is called a record. A set of records can then be said to make up a database.

The requirements of a program needed to handle a database are:

1. To allow you to enter and edit records

2. To give you a mechanism for storing the database permanently

3. To allow you to look up a specific record by specifying a field

4. Anything else you think you want!

TRY THIS

When you're designing a program of this sort the first thing you need to do is work out how the data is to be stored, what arrays are needed and so on. For example, take a record collection – space needs to be set aside for the record title, the artist, the tracks, and the date recorded. This should do to start with, but you can easily add to it later if you need to.

So let's start with the following section:

```
10  REM SET UP ARRAYS
20  DIM T$(30,15):REM 30
    RECORDS WITH T$
    HOLDING THE TITLES
30  DIM B$(30,15):
    REM ARTIST(S)
40  DIM R$(30,14,15):
    REM 14 TRACKS ON EACH
    RECORD
50  DIM D$(30,8)
60  DIM P$(15):
    REM DATABASE TITLE
65  DIM S$(15)
70  LET PTR=1:REM CURRENT
    RECORD POINTER
```

The next thing to do is to set up some kind of control menu giving you access to all the various options:

```
99   REM MENU
100  CLS
110  PRINT " DATABASE OF ";
     P$
120  PRINT
130  PRINT" 1...EDIT DATA"
140  PRINT" 2...SEARCH DATA"
150  PRINT" 3...LOAD DATA"
160  PRINT" 4...SAVE DATA"
170  PRINT" 0...END"
175  PRINT" CURRENT RECORD
     IS:";PTR
180  LET A$=INKEY$
190  IF A$="1" THEN GOSUB
     EDIT:GO TO 100
200  IF A$="2" THEN GOSUB
     SRCH:GO TO 100
210  IF A$="3" THEN GOSUB
     LOAD:GO TO 100
220  IF A$="4" THEN GOSUB
     SAVE:GO TO 100
230  IF A$="0" THEN GOSUB
     FINI:GO TO 100
240  GO TO 180
```

Notice the way we're writing the program – so far we've decided what we want to do, allowed array space for it, then approached it logically by presenting the user with a series of options, each handled by a GOSUB. As yet the program doesn't actually do anything, so we'd best get down to writing the subroutines!

Working out the works

One advantage the Spectrum has is its ability to use commands like GOSUB A, where A is set to the value of a line number. You can see the virtues of this in the section above, as you can name the subroutines with handy mnemonics. All these subroutines can now be written and then the variables set up to point to them. For instance, we'll start EDIT at 300:

```
299 REM EDIT STARTS AT 300
300 CLS
310 PRINT" EDIT MENU"
320 PRINT
330 PRINT" 1...SELECT RECORD"
340 PRINT" 2...EDIT CURRENT RECORD"
350 PRINT" 3...STEP FORWARD A RECORD"
360 PRINT" 4...STEP BACKWARD A RECORD"
370 PRINT" 0...MAIN MENU"
375 PRINT" CURRENT RECORD IS:";PTR
380 LET A$=INKEY$
390 IF A$="1" THEN GOSUB SLT:GOSUB CRR:GO TO 300
400 IF A$="2" THEN GOSUB CRR:GO TO 300
410 IF A$="3" THEN GOSUB FWD:GO TO 300
420 IF A$="4" THEN GOSUB BKD:GO TO 300
430 IF A$="0" THEN RETURN
440 GO TO 380
```

You'll have gathered by now that a good way to design programs of this type is to write the menu sections first.

Taking the simplest of the edit sections:

```
499  REM FWD (500)
     INCREMENT RECORD
     POINTER
500  LET PTR=PTR+(PTR<31)
510  RETURN
519  REM BKW (520)
     DECREMENT RECORD
     POINTER
520  LET PTR=PTR-(PTR>0)
530  RETURN
539  REM SELECT (540) A
     RECORD BY NUMBER
540  CLS
550  INPUT "ENTER RECORD
     NUMBER ";A$
560  IF VAL A$<1 OR VAL
     A$>30 THEN RETURN
570  LET PTR=VAL A$
580  RETURN
```

Now it's a question of producing the more complex field editor. Here it would be nice to have a subroutine that prints a record onto the screen, which is what the GOSUB 1000 is all about:

```
599  REM CRR FIELD EDITOR
600  GOSUB 1000:REM PRINT
     RECORD
610  INPUT "ENTER LETTER OR
     NUMBER OR FIELD TO
     EDIT. X TO END. ";A$
615  IF A$="*" THEN INPUT
     "NEW DBASE TITLE: ";P$
620  IF A$="A" THEN INPUT
     "NEW TITLE: ";
     T$(PTR):GO TO 600
630  IF A$="B" THEN INPUT
     "NEW DATE: ";D$(PTR):GO
     TO 600
640  IF A$="C" THEN INPUT
     "NEW ARTIST: ";B$(PTR)
650  IF A$="X" THEN RETURN
655  IF CODE(A$)>65 THEN GO
     TO 600
660  IF VAL (A$)<1 OR VAL
     (A$)>14 THEN GO TO 600
670  PRINT "NEW TRACK ";
     VAL(A$);":";
680  INPUT R$(PTR,VAL(A$))
690  GO TO 600
```

Now the record display

```
1000 CLS
1005 PRINT "*.DATABASE
     OF: ";P$
1006 PRINT "RECORD NUMBER:
     ";PTR
1010 PRINT "A.TITLE
     :";T$(PTR)
1020 PRINT "B.DATE :";
     D$(PTR)
1030 PRINT "C.ARTIST :";
     B$(PTR)
1040 FOR I=1 TO 20 STEP 2
1050 PRINT I;" ";
     R$(PTR,I);" ";I+1;" ";
     R$(PTR,I+1)
1060 NEXT I
1070 RETURN
```

After that we can deal with a few easy options from the same menu:

```
799  REM SAVE P$() T$()
     B$()TR$() D$()
800  INPUT "ENTER FILE
     NAME :";F$
810  SAVE F$+"P" DATA P$()
820  SAVE F$+"T" DATA T$()
830  SAVE F$+"B" DATA B$()
840  SAVE F$+"R" DATA R$()
850  SAVE F$+"D" DATA D$()
860  RETURN
899  REM LOAD P$() T$()
     B$() R$() D$()
```

```
900 INPUT "ENTER FILE
    NAME :";F$
910 LOAD F$+"P" DATA P$()
920 LOAD F$+"T" DATA T$()
930 LOAD F$+"B" DATA B$()
940 LOAD F$+"R" DATA R$()
950 LOAD F$+"D" DATA D$()
960 RETURN
```

The above could easily be converted to Microdrive by prefixing the file names with *"m";1; and this would give you a fairly fast filing system.

In search of the lost word

The final section of the program is the search routine, which looks through the entire database for a specific field and then displays the record, or records, that contain it. This is where the single record display routine comes in handy.

```
1499 REM SEARCH
1500 CLS
1510 LET PTR=1
1520 PRINT" SEARCH"
1530 PRINT
1540 INPUT " ENTER STRING
     TO BE SEARCHED FOR ";
     A$
1550 LET S$=A$
1559 REM SEARCH TITLES
1560 GOSUB 2100
1570 FOR T=1 TO 30
1580 IF S$(1 TO 15)=T$(T)
     THEN LET PTR=T:GOSUB
     1000:GOSUB 2000
1590 NEXT T
1599 REM SEARCH DATES
1600 LET S$=A$
```

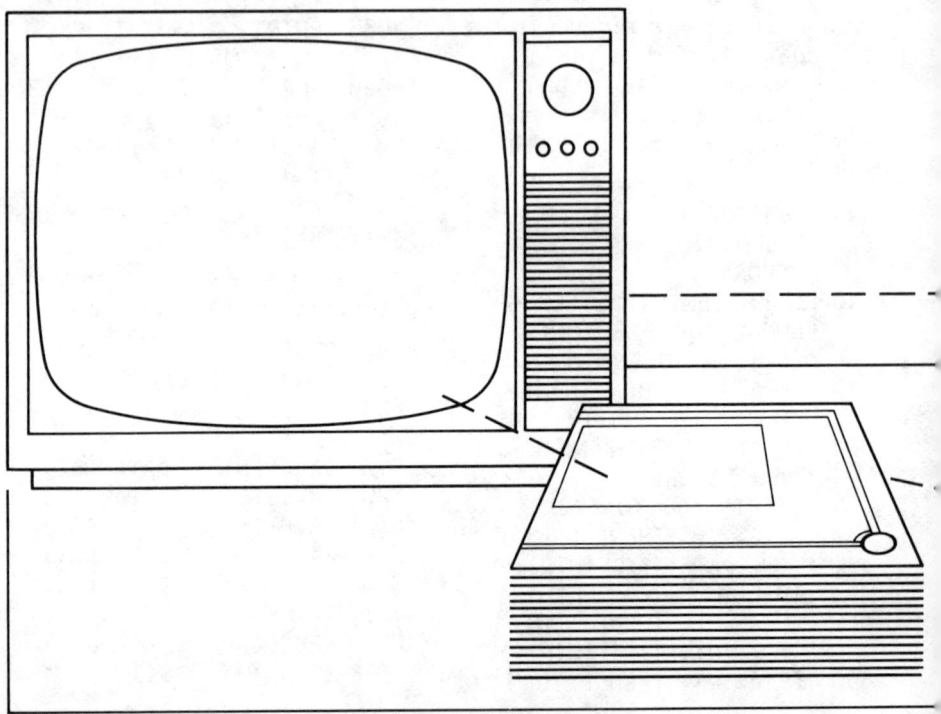

```
1610  IF LEN S$<8 THEN LET
      S$=S$+" ":GO TO 1610
1620  FOR T=1 TO 30
1630  IF S$(1 TO 8)=D$(T)
      THEN LET PTR=T:GOSUB
      1000:GOSUB 2000
1640  NEXT T
1659  REM SEARCH ARTISTS
1660  LET S$=A$
1670  GOSUB 2100
1680  FOR T=1 TO 30
1690  IF S$(1 TO 15)=A$(T)
      THEN LET PTR=T:GOSUB
      1000:GOSUB 2000
1700  NEXT T
1709  REM SEARCH TRACKS
1710  LET S$=A$
1720  GOSUB 2100
1730  FOR T=1 TO 30
1740  FOR S=1 TO 14
1750  IF S$(1 TO 15)=
      R$(T,S) THEN LET
      PTR=T:GOSUB
      1000:GOSUB 2000
1760  NEXT S:NEXT T
1770  RETURN
2000  PRINT AT 20,0;"PRESS
      SPACE TO CONTINUE"
2010  LET C$=INKEY$:IF C$<>
      " " THEN GO TO 2010
2020  RETURN
2099  REM MAKE S$ UP TO 15
      CHARS
2100  IF LEN(S$) <15 THEN
      LET S$=S$+" ":GO TO
      2100
2110  RETURN
2199  REM FINISH STARTS AT
      2200
2200  INPUT "ARE YOU
      SURE?";A$
2210  IF A$<>"Y" THEN RETURN
2220  STOP
```

You now have the makings of a primitive database, but there's still one thing you have to do. Go through the program again, and set up the variables for the GOSUBs in a new line

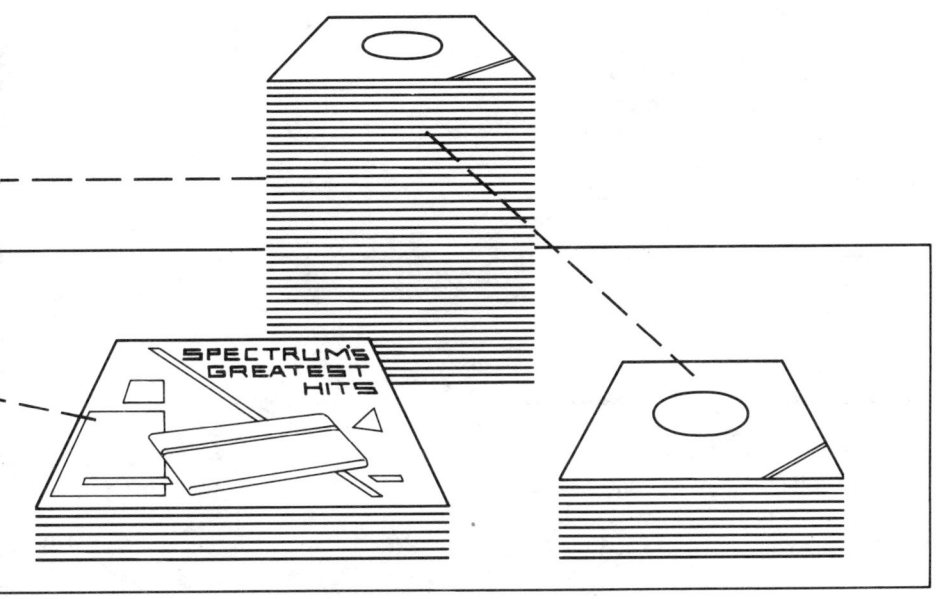

10 as follows: The EDIT section, for example, starts at 300, so you should say LET EDIT=300.

```
10  LET EDIT=300: LET
    SRCH=1500:
LET LOAD=900: LET
SAVE=800:
LET CRR=600: LET SLT=540:
LET FWD=500: LET BKD=520:
LET FINI=2200
```

The database you've got holds 30 records, and has a maximum field length of 15 characters. You can alter these numbers depending on how much memory you have available, and how long you want the data to take to load.

Checklist

In this chapter you should have learned:

- [ ] The differences between arrays and DATA statements, and the way you can use both these methods of handling information in your programs.
- [ ] How to use RESTORE.
- [ ] How to write a database program logically, using a combination of menus and GOSUBs.

Project

- [ ] Rewrite the database program so that it will catalogue a collection of books, or the addresses of your friends.

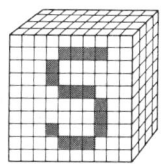

Handling arrays

One of the major uses of arrays, both numeric and string, is in adventure games. These allow you to wander around a sort of maze picking up pieces of gold and confronting various monsters.

Let's see how we can write a program that allows you to define the rooms and passageways and wander around them. As with the file handling program, the best way to start the program design is to work out what arrays will be needed.

Since the program needs a set of descriptions for the rooms etc. we need a string array to hold these. The total number of locations possible is set by the amount of memory you have available. In the program that follows this is set to 10 using the variable M. This can be increased until the memory runs out. The length of the description string is set with T; this can also be increased but it does eat up large quantities of memory. The trade off is between lots of locations with short descriptions, or less with large descriptions.

To use the description array we will also need a set of pointers to allow the rooms to be linked together in various ways. We also need to set the pointer array to default values. The following section does just this.

```
6   BORDER 3
7   INK 3
8   LET T=30
10  LET M=10
20  DIM D$(M,T)
25  DIM S(M,4)
30  DIM E(M,4)
31  LET B$="NO"
35  FOR T=1 TO M: FOR S=1
    TO 4: LET E(T,S)=-1:
    NEXT S: NEXT T
```

The next thing to do is to set out some kind of control for the program. This is the main menu and gives the options to edit the descriptions, load and save definitions, link up the rooms in a random way, and play the game. This is set out as follows:

```
40  CLS
45  DEF FN R(R)=
    INT(RND*R)+1
50  PRINT " SIMPLE
    ADVENTURE"
60  PRINT
70  PRINT " 1...PLAY"
80  PRINT " 2...EDITOR"
90  PRINT " 3...LOAD"
100 PRINT " 4...SAVE"
110 PRINT " 5...RANDOMIZE"
115 PRINT " 6...END"
120 LET A$=INKEY$:IF A$=""
    THEN GOTO 120
130 IF A$="1" THEN GOSUB
    600:GOTO 40
140 IF A$="2" THEN GOSUB
    230:GOTO 40
150 IF A$="3" THEN GOSUB
    900:GOTO 40
160 IF A$="4" THEN GOSUB
    800:GOTO 40
170 IF A$="5" THEN GOSUB
    450:GOTO 40
180 IF A$="6" THEN GOSUB
    200:GOTO 40
190 GOTO 120
```

Taking the easiest option first we will define the end option. To make sure you don't come out of the program without saving the data, it is generally a good idea to ask before doing something as drastic as stopping.

```
200 INPUT "ARE YOU SURE ";
    B$
210 IF B$="YES" THEN STOP
220 RETURN
```

The next sections are the major parts of the program. Let's take the editor first. This is again controlled from a menu giving all of the major needs to be able to define a series of locations. The menu is written in exactly the same way as the main menu; note that the REM statements are *not* used, allowing them to be removed to save space later on.

```
225 REM THIS IS THE EDITOR
230 CLS
240 PRINT "EDITOR MENU"
250 PRINT
260 PRINT "1...LIST
    LOCATIONS"
270 PRINT "2...EDIT
    LOCATION"
280 PRINT "3...MAIN MENU"
290 LET A$=INKEY$
300 IF A$="1" THEN GOSUB
    340:GOTO 230
310 IF A$="2" THEN GOSUB
    410:GOTO 230
320 IF A$="3" THEN GOSUB
    1000:RETURN
330 GOTO 290
```

Taking these options in order, here is a routine to list the locations that have, or haven't, been defined. Obviously if there are a large number of locations it's a good idea to allow some kind of escape mechanism to get back to the previous menu.

```
335  REM LIST LOCATIONS
340  PRINT "HIT 'S' TO STOP"
350  FOR T=1 TO M
360  PRINT T;"==>";D$(T)
365  PRINT "EXITS ARE ";
366  FOR S=1 TO 4:PRINT
     ("NORTH " AND E(T,S)=0
     AND S=1);("SOUTH " AND
     E(T,S)=0 AND S=2);
     ("EAST " AND E(T,S)=0
     AND S=3);("WEST " AND
     E(T,S)=0 AND S=4);:
     NEXT S
367  PRINT
370  LET A$=INKEY$
380  IF A$="S" THEN LET T=M
390  NEXT T
400  RETURN
```

One of the clever things about the Spectrum's Basic is the ability to perform the print statement in line 366 allowing the exits to be printed only if they have been specified by putting a zero in the 'E' array.

This direction specification is performed in the edit location section that follows. This just asks for the location number and then expects a set of exit directions. These are 'north', 'south', 'east', and 'west'. Directions such as 'up', and 'down' etc. can be added by changing the DIM in line 25 and 30 to allow space in the E and S arrays.

```
405  REM EDIT LOCATION
410  INPUT "ENTER LOCATION
     TO EDIT ";L
420  PRINT D$(L)
430  INPUT"==>";D$(L)
431  INPUT "Enter exits
     n/s/e/w ";A$
```

After entering information you don't need to use it all. The next section checks the entries and puts them in the correct positions on the 'E' array. North being E(T,1), South being E(T,2) and East and West being 3 and 4 respectively. Using this routine allows the exits to be entered in the wrong order without confusing the program.

```
432  FOR T=1 TO 4
433  FOR S=1 TO LEN A$
434  LET E(L,T)=((A$(S TO
     S)="N") AND T=1)+
     ((A$(S TO S)="S") AND
     T=2)+((A$(S TO S)="E")
     AND T=3)+((A$(S TO
     S)="W") AND T=4)-1
435  IF E(L,T)=0 THEN LET
     S=5
437  NEXT S:NEXT T
440  RETURN
```

Once all the locations have been defined and described they need to be attached to each other. Normally, an adventure will have these predefined as part of the game. Since this is a simple adventure and contains no moveable objects we have to make it exciting somehow. This is done by allowing locations to be attached randomly to each other but making sure that if you exit south, then you must enter north.

```
444  REM JUGGLER
450  GOSUB 1060
455  FOR T=1 TO M
460  FOR S=1 TO 4
470  IF E(T,S)=-1 THEN
     GOTO 500
```

```
480 IF E(T,S)<>0 THEN
    GOTO 500
490 GOSUB 520
500 NEXT S
510 RETURN
```

The juggler routine is split into three main parts. The first is a subroutine that resets the original directions into the E array (subroutine 1060). The juggler then goes through the locations and checks whether they have any valid exits. If they contain 0, an exit, the routine jumps down to line 520 and roots through 100 random locations until one is found that fits the bill of matching North for South, East to West etc. The location numbers are then swapped over in the E array, making a connection.

```
515 REM SWAP EXITS
520 FOR U=1 TO 100
530 LET V=FN R(M)
540 IF (S=1 AND E(V,2)<>0)
    OR (S=2 AND E(V,1)<>0)
    OR (S=3 AND E(V,4)<>0)
    OR (S=4 AND E(V,3)<>0)
    THEN GOTO 570
545 LET E(V,(S=2)+
    ((S=1)*2) + ((S=3)*4)+
    ((S=4)*3))=T
550 LET E(T,S)=V:LET U=100
570 NEXT U
580 RETURN
```

When all the locations have been covered, the routine returns to the main menu.

The next major section of the program allows the adventure to be run. First the description of location one is displayed and then the exits are given. After entering the direction to be followed, lines 640 and 650 work out whether the direction is valid or whether it has not been assigned. Line 680 assigns the new location number to L, the correct position.

```
599  REM MAIN GAME
600  LET L=1
605  PRINT D$(L)
620  PRINT "EXITS ARE ";
     ("NORTH" AND E(L,1)
     <>-1);(" SOUTH" AND
     E(L,2)<>-1);(" EAST" AND
     E(L,3)<>-1);(" WEST"
     AND E(L,4)<>-1)
625  PRINT A$;" _____
     _____"
630  INPUT "WHICH WAY ";A$
635  LET A$=A$(1 TO 1)
640  IF (A$="N" AND E(L,1)=
     -1) OR (A$="S" AND
     E(L,2)=-1) OR (A$="E"
     AND E(L,3)=-1) OR
     (A$="W" AND E(L,4)=-1)
     THEN PRINT "SORRY, YOU
     CAN'T GO THAT WAY":
     GOTO 620
650  IF (A$="N" AND E(L,1)=
     0) OR (A$="S" AND
     E(L,2)=0) OR (A$="E"
     AND E(L,3)=0) OR
     (A$="W" AND E(L,4)=0)
     THEN PRINT"YOU
     ARE IN THE
     WILDERNESS, YOU'D BEST
     GO BACK": GOTO 610
660  IF A$="F" THEN GOSUB
     700
670  IF B$="YES" THEN RETURN
680  IF A$="L" THEN GOTO 610
682  LET L=((A$="N")*E(L,1))
     +((A$="S")*E(L,2))+
     ((A$="E")*E(L,3))+
     ((A$="W")*E(L,4))
685  IF L=0 THEN PRINT "EH
     ??":LET L=1
690  GOTO 610
```

The other options are L which reprints the current description, and F which allows you to get back to the main menu. Again, to make the program as idiot-proof as possible, it is a good idea to ask whether the player would like to end or not with:

```
700  INPUT "ARE YOU SURE ";
     B$
710  RETURN
799  REM SAVE D$() E() S()
```

The final subroutines are generally concerned with data handling, and allow the main game array to be saved and loaded from tape or microdrive.

```
800  INPUT "ENTER ADVENTURE
     FILE NAME ";F$
815  SAVE *"m";1;F$+"S"
     DATA S()
820  SAVE *"m";1;F$+"D"
     DATA D$()
830  SAVE *"m";1;F$+"P"
     DATA E()
840  RETURN
899  REM LOAD S() E() D$()
900  INPUT "ENTER FILE
     NAME ";F$
910  LOAD *"M";1;F$+"S"
     DATA S()
915  LOAD *"M";1;F$+"D"
     DATA D$()
920  LOAD *"M";1;F$+"P"
     DATA E()
930  RETURN
```

Since the juggler program alters the E array, to re-juggle the program the directions need to be saved somewhere. The following two routines load and save the E array in the S array (S for save).

```
 999 REM STORE ORIGINAL
     DIRECTIONS
1000 FOR T=1 TO M
1010 FOR S=1 TO 4
1020 LET S(T,S)=E(T,S)
1030 NEXT S
1040 NEXT T
1050 RETURN
1059 REM RETRIEVE ORIGINAL
     DIRECTIONS
1060 FOR T=1 TO M
1070 FOR S=1 TO 4
1080 LET E(T,S)=S(T,S)
1090 NEXT S
1100 NEXT T
1110 RETURN
```

And that's it. You can probably think of hundreds of improvements to this, and it has been written in such a way as to allow these to be entered with ease. The art of using the program to define a good adventure is to make the locations interesting enough so that they stand up on their own. If you want to provide monsters then simply enter a description such as:

You stand in a dank dark closet. From the corner comes a piercing shriek which dies away into a whimpering moan.

Checklist

In this chapter you should have learned:

- [ ] How the Spectrum can handle multiple arrays, and how you can make them relate to one another.

- [ ] To make sure your REM statements come in the line before a subroutine starts, so that they don't interfere with your reading of the program.

- [ ] How AND can be used to sort through possible options in a program.

- [ ] The way to use random GOSUBs to bring an element of chance into the program.

Project

- [ ] Try adding a section that allows you to pick up pieces of treasure to the program.

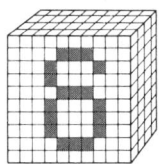

Introduction to graphics

The Spectrum's graphics facilities are fairly easy to use – graphics are much more complicated on many home micros. On the Spectrum graphics basically fall into two categories – user-defined graphics, which are based on the 32×22 character positions available on the Spectrum's screen, and the PLOT and DRAW group of commands that allow you to produce graphics down to individual picture elements, or pixels. The Spectrum has 255×176 of these.

But there's one major disadvantage to graphics on the Spectrum. You can only set INK and PAPER colours down to individual character positions, not to pixels, and, while you can get round this if you remember it, you can make a dreadful mess of the screen if you get your sums wrong.

TRY THIS

Let's say you want to draw a grid on the Spectrum's screen, you'd possibly use something like this:

```
10 CLS
20 FOR N=5 TO 253 STEP 8
30 INK 5: PLOT N,0: DRAW 0,175
40 NEXT N
50 FOR N=5 TO 173 STEP 8
60 INK 6: PLOT 0,N: DRAW 255,0
70 NEXT N
80 GO TO 20
```

What you should have here is a program that draws coloured lines vertically on the screen, then draws horizontal lines across them in a different colour. But as the second group of lines is going through the character positions occupied by the first group of lines, it resets the INK colour of those lines to the new INK colour.

You'll get the same effect whatever screen handling commands you use, so even if you're using user-defined

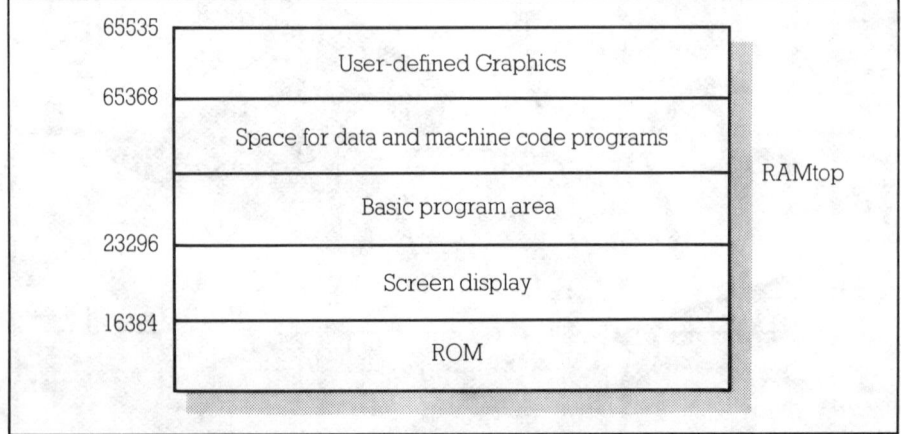

graphics you'll find that anything in another INK colour being drawn in that position will change a graphic's colour. Usually this is a problem, but there are instances when it can be useful.

Let's say you design an 'invaders' type game, using PLOT and DRAW to deal with the lasers. If a white laser beam enters the invader's character position it could be used to turn the alien white before you make it disappear or explode.

Displays defined

It's all very well to be able to draw pictures and fill them, and there's no great problem saving them on tape as a SCREEN$, but you'll have noticed how long it takes to reload a picture. This is fine if you want a display on the screen while a long game is loading, but if you wanted to call up a series of pictures within a game it'd be useless.

It's at this point that it becomes handy to learn a little about how the Spectrum organises its memory. The diagram here shows part of the Spectrum's memory map – for more information you should refer to chapter 24 of the Spectrum manual. The 48K Spectrum has 65,536 memory locations altogether, and you can think of these as boxes that can store numbers.

Each of these addresses can hold one byte, which is a number from 0–255. Now think about the way you define user-defined graphics – each line of the graphic defined contains an eight digit binary number from 00000000 to 11111111 which, if you convert it to decimal, is somewhere from 0–255.

Now you can store numbers of this order in *all* memory locations, not just in the locations that deal with user-defined graphics – chapter 25 of the Spectrum manual shows you what is actually stored in the memory area from 23552 to 23733, and what you can do by varying this.

Most of the area above 23296 consists of the Basic program area, which stretches up to RAMtop, beyond which you find the user-defined graphics. A Basic program will not interfere with anything stored above RAMtop (literally, the *top* of Random Access Memory), so it's possible to store information above this point, and provided your Basic program doesn't POKE any new numbers into this area it's possible to call up machine code routines from Basic.

TRY THIS

As you're about to find out, the Spectrum's screen display is organised in a bizarre and unnerving fashion – don't worry too much about this yet, as we'll show you how to get round it shortly!

```
10 FOR N=16384 TO 23295
20 POKE N,INT(RND*256)
30 NEXT N
```

Ask yourself what we're doing here – the memory locations from 16384 to 22528 control the screen display, or display file. We're POKEing a random number from 0–255 into each of these locations, and this is ultimately producing a combination of dot pattern and colour on each of the character positions on the screen. Depending on your taste, the effect is either colourful or gruesome!

But you'll notice that the Spectrum draws the screen oddly, in small sections, and finally inks in the colour. This is because of the slightly odd way it stores the screen information in memory. If you add 40 GO TO 40, incidentally, you'll suppress the report line at the bottom of the screen, and you'll find your display remains 26 lines deep rather than reverting to 24 when the report comes up. You can't actually produce a display on the two report lines from Basic.

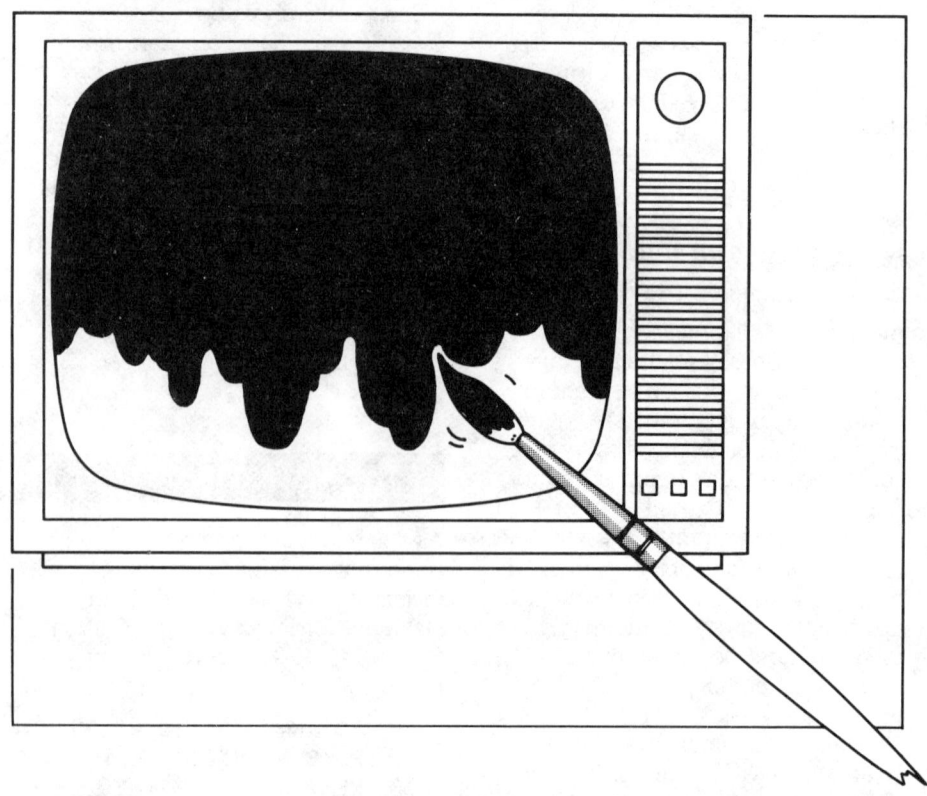

Storing your treasures

From what you've learned so far it should be clear how you can store and recall a screen display. As the status of the display is held as numbers from 0–255 in locations 16384–22528, all you need is a routine that reads these numbers, stores them elsewhere in memory, and calls them back when you need them.

But think of the practicalities before you write it – this will be a routine you'll want to use repeatedly, and although it could be done in Basic you'd then have to write it into all your Basic programs. So what do you do?

TRY THIS

It's possible to decrease the size of the Basic program area by moving RAMtop down. This leaves you more space for machine code programs which, with the qualifications we dealt with above, do not interfere with Basic programs.

```
10 CLEAR 58430
20 FOR N=58431 TO 58450
30 READ B: POKE N,B:
   NEXT N
40 DATA 33,0,64,17,83,228,
   24,6,33,83,228,17,0,
   64,1,0,27,237,176,201
50 NEW
```

What you've got here is a program that brings RAMtop down to 58430 and POKEs a machine code program into the area above this. It then NEWs itself, removing the Basic program lines, but leaving the machine code above RAMtop.

You can now draw your screen as you wish, and call the routine to store it with LET screen=USR 58431. You call the screen back with LET screen= USR 58439. The screen itself is stored in the 6912 addresses from 58451 on. This number 6912 comes from the calculation of eight lines per character position×32 columns×24 rows plus 32×24 for the attributes of each character position.

You can use any variable you like instead of 'screen', but bear in mind that it should not be a variable used in a Basic program you're running.

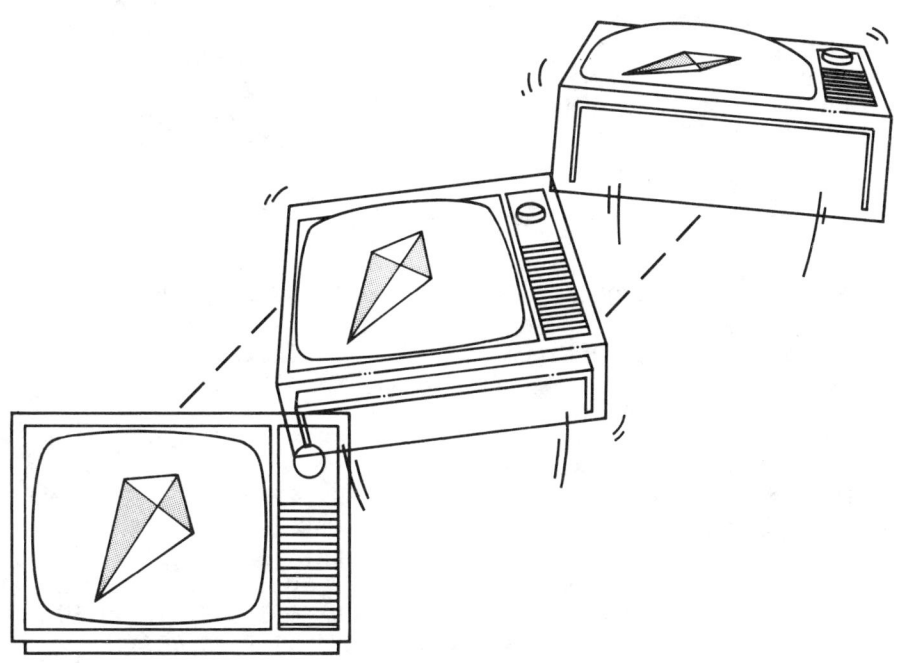

Introduction to graphics

One of the more useful graphics routines that is not provided on the Spectrum is the ability to fill shapes. There are a number of methods of doing this, most of which are fairly slow in Basic.

The following routine is called the 'grassfire fill'. From a specified point inside the area to be filled, the routine checks four adjacent points to see if they have been filled. If they're not, then they are filled and their locations are saved in two arrays (one for the X and one for the Y positions). This filling continues until all the points inside the area have been filled. The boundary can be thought of as a trench dug around the area which stops the spread of the fire.

The size of the area to be filled is limited by the size of the array used to hold the adjacent points. This has the disadvantage that the size is limited to about a 200×200 point square. The advantage is that not too much memory is taken up and in the machine code version you are sure of the routine stopping eventually.

Try this and note how slow it is:

```
10   LET A=200:REM SIZE OF
     POINT ARRAY
20   DIM X(A):DIM Y(A)
30   CIRCLE 100,100,30
40   LET X=105:LET Y=105
50   GOSUB 1000:REM FILL
60   STOP
999  REM GRASSFIRE FILL
     STARTING AT X,Y
1000 LET P1=1:LET P2=2
1010 LET X(1)=X:LET Y(1)=Y
1020 FOR D=1 TO 4
1030 LET T=-(D=1)+(D=3):
     LET S=-(D=4)+(D=2)
1040 LET PX=X(P1)+T: LET
     PY=Y(P1)+S
1050 IF POINT (PX,PY)=1
     THEN GOTO 1100
1060 PLOT PX,PY
1070 LET X(P2)=PX:LET
     Y(P2)=PY
1080 LET P2=P2+1
1090 IF P2>A THEN LET P2=1
1100 NEXT D
1110 LET P1=P1+1
1120 IF P1>A THEN LET P1=1
1130 IF P1<>P2 THEN GOTO
     1020
1140 RETURN
```

Now enter the next routine and save the machine code to tape, or microdrive, with:

SAVE "FILL" CODE 30519,173

or

SAVE *"M";1;"FILL" CODE 30519,168

```
5   REM MACHINE CODE
    VERSION OF GRASSFIRE
10  CLEAR 30000
15  LET C=0
20  FOR T=30519 TO
    30519+168
30  READ A:POKE T,A
40  LET C=C+A
50  NEXT T
60  IF C<>15116 THEN
    PRINT"CHECKSUM ERROR?
    CHECK YOUR DATA
    STATEMENTS."
70  PRINT"POKE 30514 WITH X
    LOC"
80  PRINT"POKE 30515 WITH Y
    LOC"
90  PRINT"EXECUTE WITH RAND
    USR 30519"
100 DATA 62,0,50,48,119,62,
    1,50,49,119
110 DATA 33,48,117,58,50,
    119,119,33,48,118
```

```
120 DATA 58,51,119,119,62,4,
    50,52,119,33
130 DATA 48,117,58,48,119,
    95,22,0,25,78
140 DATA 33,48,118,25,70,
    58,52,119,254,1
150 DATA 202,130,119,254,
    2,202,126,119,254,3
160 DATA 202,122,119,13,
    195,131,119,4,195,131
170 DATA 119,12,195,131,119,
    5,120,50,54,119
180 DATA 121,50,53,119,58,
    54,119,71,58,53
190 DATA 119,79,205,206,34,
    205,213,45,254,1
200 DATA 202,198,119,58,54,
    119,71,58,53,119
210 DATA 79,205,229,34,33,
    48,117,58,49,119
220 DATA 95,22,0,25,58,53,
    119,119,33,48
230 DATA 118,25,58,54,119,
    119,58,49,119,60
240 DATA 50,49,119,58,52,
    119,61,50,52,119
250 DATA 194,84,119,58,48,
    119,60,50,48,119
260 DATA 71,58,49,119,184,
    194,79,119,201,75
270 DATA 69,78,78
```

Watch how much faster machine code is in this program:

```
10 CLEAR 30000
20 LOAD *"M";1;"FILL" CODE
   30519:REM MICRODRIVE
   LOAD, STRIP OFF *"M";1;
   FOR CASSETTE
30 CIRCLE 100,100,30
40 POKE 30514,100
50 POKE 30515,100
60 RANDOMIZE USR 30519
70 PRINT"NEAT EH?"
```

Memory location 30514 is used to hold the horizontal position of a point inside the shape, and 30515 holds the vertical position. Calling the routine at 30519 runs the machine code.

The CLEAR 30000, at the beginning of the program, not only sets aside some memory area for the machine code, it reserves memory for the arrays.

The machine code routine works in exactly the same way as the Basic program but, as you can see, is quite a lot faster.

You will be able to fill any shape with this routine. The only thing to be careful of is to make sure that the edge of the area has no gaps in it as this will lead to the fire spreading outside the required area.

Checklist

In this chapter you should have learned:

- [ ] How the Spectrum organises its screen, and how the picture on the screen is stored in memory.
- [ ] A little about the Spectrum's memory map, and how to make space for machine code by using CLEAR.
- [ ] How to take a picture from the screen, store it above RAMtop, then call it back at will.

Project

- [ ] Write a drawing program that includes a Basic routine to read the attributes of every character position on the screen, and then change the colour – see ATTR in the Spectrum manual for help.

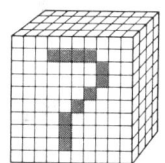

Advanced colour

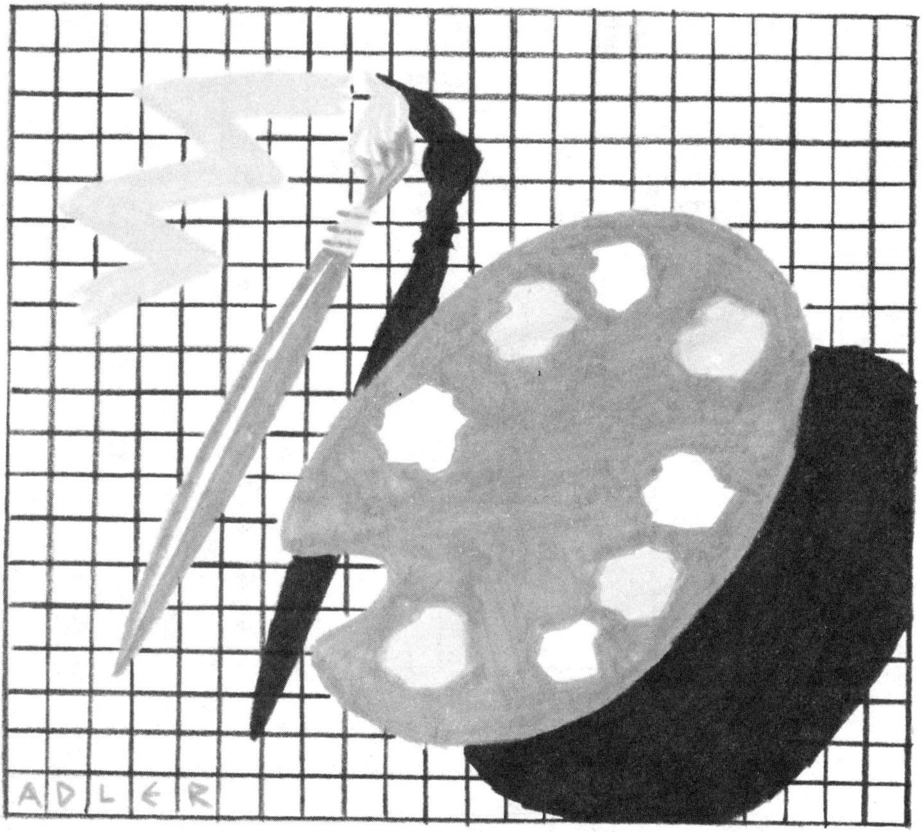

If you've tried to draw detailed pictures with your Spectrum, and if you've also seen the title screens of some of the more spectacular commercial games around, you'll probably have asked yourself how programmers do it. These games apparently have highly detailed opening screens where individual pixels are marked in separate colours.

Now as you're probably aware the Spectrum is perfectly happy having individual pixels set as INK and PAPER colours, but it has the limitation that you can only set one INK and one PAPER colour for each character position – so how is it done?

The short answer is that it isn't done this way. It may seem disappointing that you can't alter this, but the fact that superb pictorial screens *are* possible on the Spectrum shows that, with a little ingenuity, you can get round the problem.

Really it's all a matter of drawing your pictures so that your lines fit easily into character positions – take a look at the diagram here to see how it should be done.

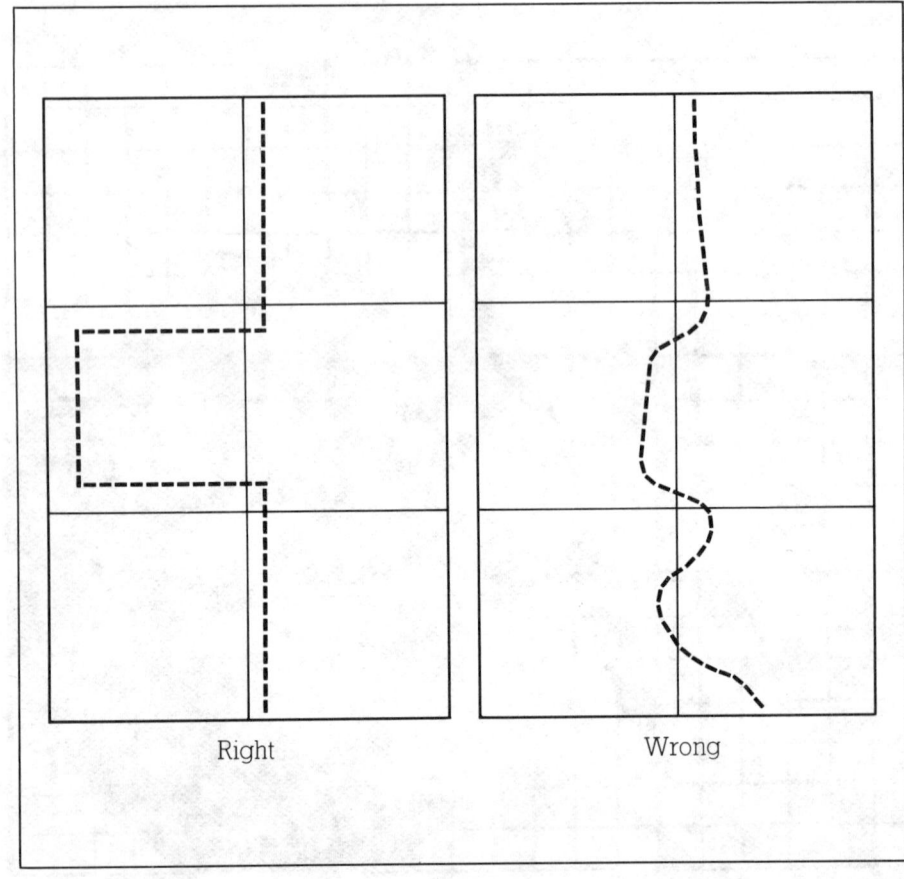

Right   Wrong

Drawing on experience

You already have a routine to fill in the shapes you've drawn, but PLOTting and DRAWing on the Spectrum can be fairly tedious, and it's easy to make mistakes. What you really need is a way to DRAW shapes easily, one that allows you to rub out your mistakes. Naturally you'll want to use colour in this routine, so you'll also need a way to check when you're going out of a character position's boundaries. If you can see this on the screen it'll stop you making too many messy mistakes:

```
10  LET INK=1: LET X=128:
    LET Y=88
20  LET GRID=200:
    LET REPORT=900:
    LET PRINT=300:
    LET STOP=500
30  GOSUB GRID:REM SET UP
    GRID
40  GOSUB REPORT:REM SET
    UP PRINTING IN REPORT
    LINES
49  REM SET UP MODES
50  IF INKEY$="I" THEN LET
    INK=1: GOSUB PRINT
60  IF INKEY$="O" THEN LET
    INK=3: GOSUB PRINT
70  IF INKEY$="P" THEN LET
    INK=0
75  GOSUB PRINT
80  IF INKEY$="S" THEN
    GOSUB STOP
99  REM MOVE CURSOR
100 IF INKEY$="A" THEN LET
    X=X-1
110 IF INKEY$="D" THEN LET
    X=X+1
120 IF INKEY$="W" THEN LET
    Y=Y+1
130 IF INKEY$="X" THEN LET
    Y=Y-1
140 IF INKEY$="Q" THEN LET
    X=X-1: LET Y=Y+1
150 IF INKEY$="E" THEN LET
    X=X+1: LET Y=Y+1
160 IF INKEY$="Z" THEN LET
    X=X-1: LET Y=Y-1
170 IF INKEY$="C" THEN LET
    X=X+1: LET Y=Y-1
180 GO TO 50
```

In this program key in INK as I, N and K; and key in PRINT and STOP in the same way. They are variable names *not* key words.

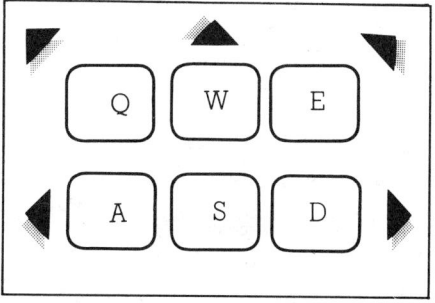

What we have here follows the usual format. With the exception of lines 100–170, which activate an eight-direction cursor cluster around the S key, the program so far consists of GOSUBs. You'll notice, however, that there's a GOSUB for the menu (GOSUB REPORT), and this is a new diversion.

There's a perfectly logical reason for this. What we're producing here is a graphics design program, so you'll want to use the whole of the screen for drawing on. If you have your menu printed on the screen you'll find you don't have the whole of it to draw on, so the tidiest way of dealing with the problem is by using the report lines, which aren't available from Basic, and clearly it would be foolish to tackle that part of the program first!

Hold onto your hat though – we're going to tackle that bit second.

Before we do, take a look at the other subroutines we'll be writing. The grid routine is fairly plain sailing. What we'll do is produce a chessboard pattern that will show the boundaries of the character positions all over the screen. INK and PAPER are obvious enough, showing you whether you're drawing a line or skipping, while STOP will give you an elegant way of bringing the whole show to a halt, while PRINT will mess around with POINT to sort out whether or not the image is on the screen.

The menu

You've already seen how you can get an image on the bottom two lines of the screen by POKEing numbers into the relevant parts of the display file – this may seem a tedious way to do things, but bear in mind that some micros make you use POKE to print on all the screen.

Still, you're probably wondering how you work out the numbers you should POKE into each location – sounds tedious, doesn't it? Fortunately it isn't. It's all a matter of looking in the ROM for the dot patterns of what you want to PRINT, then POKEing this number into the part of screen memory dealing with the character position you want to PRINT at.

You could simplify this further by working out the necessary DATA you'd need to POKE in, then just POKEing it in with a FOR...NEXT loop, but we're not going to do this right now, as the problem with DATA statements is the fact that nobody but the author understands them. And besides that, the following subroutine, apart from making the author's head hurt while he was working it out, allows you to print any characters you like in the report lines. Just change what's written in A$:

```
899 REM PRINT IN REPORT
    LINES - REPORT=900
900 DIM A$(61)
910 LET A$="MODE = DRAW
    CURSOR = 128,88 PRESS
    D FOR DRAW, S FOR
    SKIP"
920 FOR N=1 TO 61
930 LET B=CODE A$(N)
940 LET C=15360+B*8
950 LET D=20671+N
960 FOR P=0 TO 7
970 POKE D+(256*P),PEEK
    (C+P)
980 NEXT P:NEXT N
990 RETURN
```

If you want to see this program in action add a PAUSE 0 line at 985 – this will freeze the screen until you press a key. Now exactly what are we doing here? Lines 900 and 910 are fairly obvious, dimensioning a 61 character string array and defining it. Make sure the string you type in has 61 characters, by the way, otherwise you'll get an error message.

Line 920 begins a FOR...NEXT loop which first obtains the CODE of the character you're on, then defines C as 15360 plus eight times that CODE. The address in memory where the Spectrum's character set starts is 15360, and as each character has eight lines of dot patterns, taking up eight addresses, the start address of any given character is eight times its CODE plus 15360.

Now we know where the character starts we have to find out where to put it on the screen. Address 20672 is the address of the first row of pixels for the first character in line 22 of the screen, and, as for each character position the eight addresses go up in stages of 256, you have to POKE your number into D, then into D+256, then D+512 and so on. This is what the first part of line 970 does.

But just to keep you on your toes the ROM character set is stored in consecutive addresses, so the second part of 970 PEEKs these. You then move onto the next character, and the next character position by adding 1 to D, as the first address of the next character position is 1 higher than last. You might be forgiven for asking what maniac devised the screen memory!

Row:	Column:						
	1	2	3	4	5	6	7
	16384	16385	16386	16387	16388	16389	16390
	16640	16641	16642	16643	16644	16645	16646
	16896	16897	16898	16899	16900	16901	16902
	17152	17153	17154	17155	17156	17157	17158
	17408	17409	17410	17411	17412	17413	17414
	17664	17665	17666	17667	17668	17669	17670
	17920	17921	17922	17923	17924	17925	17926
	18176	18177	18178	18179	18180	18181	18182

The table here shows the way the first seven characters in the first line of the screen display are laid out in memory. Notice how the memory addresses go up in ones when you're reading across the screen from left to right, but that the second row of addresses seems to be out of order. If the Spectrum screen was organised in what we would say was a logical way, we'd have 32 numbers along the screen (to handle 32 character positions), so the first number of the second row of pixels should be 16384+32, ie 16416.

Now if you hunt down in screen memory you'll find that 16416 is the address of the first row of pixels of the character position 1,0, and if you go back to our screen filling program you'll see the Spectrum draws a screen one row of pixels at a time through the first eight rows of character positions, then the second row, and on to the eighth. It then moves on to the next eight rows, and finally does the last (which include the two report lines).

You'll therefore see that any routine that did a simple thing like PEEK the locations for one character position, then POKE them into another would be quite convoluted.

If you want to be able to POKE to any part of the screen the table overleaf will show you where to do it:

Display memory map

LINE	START OF LINE	END OF LINE
0	16384	16415
1	16416	16447
2	16448	16479
3	16480	16511
4	16512	16543
5	16544	16575
6	16576	16607
7	16608	16639
8	18432	18463
9	18464	18495
10	18496	18527
11	18528	18559
12	18560	18591
13	18592	18623
14	18624	18655
15	18656	18687
16	20480	20511
17	20512	20543
18	20544	20575
19	20576	20607
20	20608	20639
21	20640	20671
22	20672	20703
23	20704	20735

You'll notice that there is a system of sorts to the screen memory. The start of each line is 32 addresses above the start of the previous line, except in the case of the jump between lines 15 and 16, where you have to add 1824.

The cursor

The location of the cursor is probably the most important part of the program, because if you can't judge when you're leaving a given character position you'll wind up with the most unholy mess when you come to fill your drawings in. Normally you'd think of a cursor as a flashing square or as a cross shape, but for this specialised purpose you really need something that shows the boundaries of the square you're on.

So you could organise it as a dot with a line drawn around the character position it's currently in. But you'd have to move this box before the cursor came into contact with it or it would spoil your drawing, and this would be quite fiddly. For the same reason anything involving INK colour would be difficult to manage as two rival INKs in the same character position will cause chaos.

Which leads us on to PAPER. If we POKE cyan PAPER attributes into every second character position on the screen, we'll wind up with a blue and white chess board pattern. You can draw over this as much as you like, then, when you're finished, toggle it off and use the fill routine you collected earlier.

```
199 REM SET UP GRID -
    GRID=200
200 FOR N=22528 TO 23168
    STEP 64
210 FOR P=0 TO 31 STEP 2
220 POKE N+P,40: POKE
    N+P+33,40
230 NEXT P:NEXT N
240 RETURN
```

Here N is again dealing with memory locations, this time the area used to store the attributes of a given character position. Each of these memory locations stores a specific number for a combination of INK, PAPER, BRIGHT and FLASH, so it's just a matter of writing a routine to POKE them into the right positions.

The table here shows the relevant addresses for each position:

Attribute screen memory map

LINE	START OF LINE	END OF LINE
0	22528	22559
1	22560	22591
2	22592	22623
3	22624	22655
4	22656	22687
5	22688	22719
6	22720	22751
7	22752	22783

8	22784	22815
9	22816	22847
10	22848	22879
11	22880	22911
12	22912	22943
13	22944	22975
14	22976	23007
15	23008	23039
16	23040	23071
17	23072	23103
18	23104	23135
19	23136	23167
20	23168	23199
21	23200	23231
22	23232	23263
23	23264	23295

The only thing left to do is to produce a method of altering the mode indicator in the report line. It would be possible to incorporate it in our earlier routine for printing in these lines, but not doing this doesn't add much to the program:

```
299 REM PRINT
300 PLOT INK INK;X,Y
399 REM CHANGE WINDOW
400 IF INK=1 THEN LET
    A$="DRAW"
410 IF INK=0 THEN LET
    A$="SKIP"
420 FOR N=1 TO 4
430 LET B=CODE A$(N)
440 LET C=15360+B*8
450 LET D=20678+N
460 FOR P=0 TO 7
470 POKE D+(256*P),PEEK
    (C+P)
480 NEXT P:NEXT N
490 RETURN
```

We could also tidy up the stop routine.

```
499 REM STOP
500 FOR N=22528 TO 23199
510 POKE N,56
520 NEXT N:STOP
```

Adding colour

Once you've got to grips with the Spectrum's screen memory, producing colour is relatively easy. Provided you've got your INK colours in the right character positions, it's just a matter of altering the attributes of the character positions you want to colour. The table below shows you what you should POKE in for each combination of effects.

You should also be able to put the drawing program together with the fill program to produce quite a convincing graphics program. Of course there are plenty of things it can't do – in particular, it'd make life a lot easier if you could magnify the character position the cursor was on so you could see individual pixels, but this could be added.

Paper				Ink				
	Black	Blue	Red	Magenta	Green	Cyan	Yellow	White
Black	0	1	2	3	4	5	6	7
Blue	8	9	10	11	12	13	14	15
Red	16	17	18	19	20	21	22	23
Magenta	24	25	26	27	28	29	30	31
Green	32	33	34	35	36	37	38	39
Cyan	40	41	42	43	44	45	46	47
Yellow	48	49	50	51	52	53	54	55
White	56	57	58	59	60	61	62	63

If you want a character BRIGHT then you add 64 to the attributes above, and FLASH is obtained by adding a further 128.

Checklist

In this chapter you should have learned:

- [ ] How to avoid making a mess of the screen through clashes of DRAW and INK and PAPER.

- [ ] How to work out where to POKE in screen memory to get an image on the screen, and where else to POKE to colour it.

- [ ] How to read dot patterns from ROM.

Projects

- [ ] Write a new subroutine to change the attributes for the whole screen in any way the user wishes.

- [ ] Write a typewriter routine that takes what you key in and prints it in the report lines.

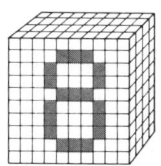

The system variables

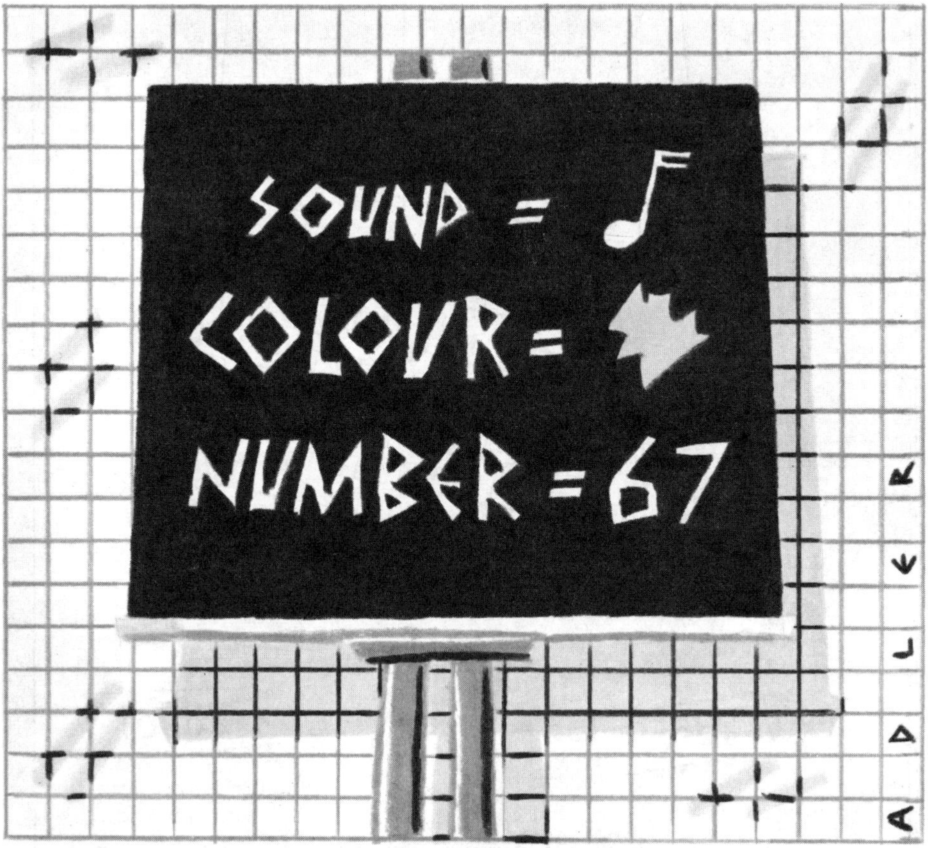

The system variables are what the computer uses to do its house keeping. Such things as keeping track of the current Basic program line, and the state of the keyboard are all stored in the system variables memory between 23552 and 23732. All of these variables are available for the user to read but not all of them are writeable, since doing so can cause the system to crash. Generally the crash is caused by not knowing exactly what the location is used for and POKEing something into it at the wrong time.

Some of the variables can be very useful and allow the Spectrum to be tailored to suit a particular need, such as completely redefining the character set or writing on the status lines.

To avoid unexpected results, turn off, and then on, your Spectrum between using the following routines.

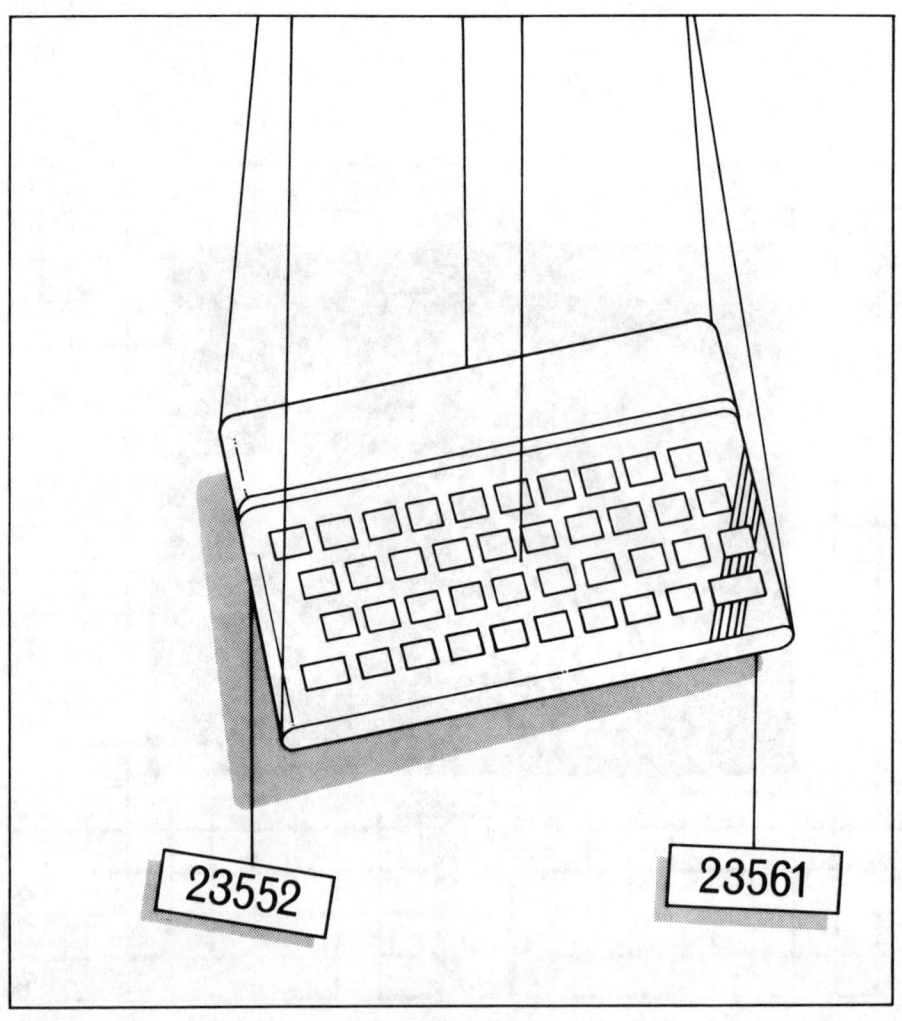

The following list gives some details on the more useful variables and some ideas of what they can be used for.

Before starting on these, there are a couple of useful functions you can have at your finger tips. The first allows a two byte address to be PEEKed from memory. This is:

```
DEF FN A(X)=PEEK X+256*PEEK (X+1)
```

and, as you will see later, it comes in very handy when exploring pointers that point to pointers.

To split a number (N) into its high and low components, use the following method:

```
HI=INT(N/256)
LO=N-256*INT(N/256)
```

This will also be used quite a lot later on since most of the pointers in the system variables are held as two bytes, allowing addresses and line numbers between 0 and 65535 to be pointed to. Some of the system variables are either so transitory or just plain useless to us that they are not worth bothering with for Basic routines. Some of the ones not covered may be of use to machine code programmers but since this is a little beyond the scope of this book, you should look elsewhere for the details.

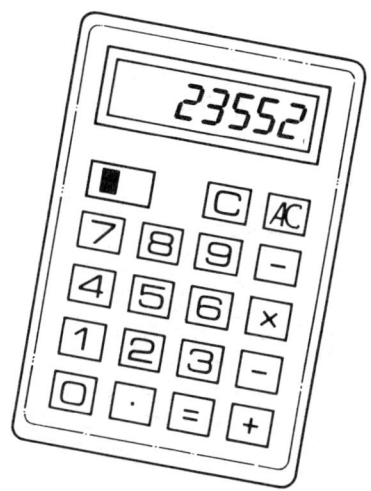

four locations take over but have the same functions. Taking the top set:

23556 contains 255 if no key is being pressed, otherwise it holds the ASCII code of the upper case letter of the key.

23557 holds the current key repeat speed counter, normally 5 and copied from 23562.

23558 holds the delay number between the press of the key and the repeat time. This value is obtained from 23561 and is normally 35. It counts down to 0 before the key repeats.

23559 contains the lower case ASCII code of the key currently being pressed.

23552 KSTATE

The locations from 23552 to 23559 are used by the system for scanning the keyboard. They are split into two sets of four bytes. The second set is used to control the detection of the first key pressed. If another key is held down, and the first then released, the first

23560 LASTK

This location is used by the keyboard scan routine to store the ASCII value of the last key that was pressed. It could be PEEKed instead of using INKEY$, obviating the need to use CODE.

69
The system variables

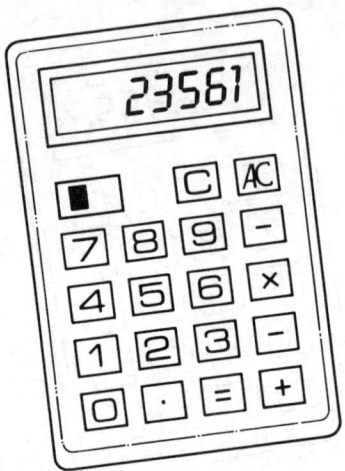

being evaluated. For example:

```
10 FOR T=FN X(0) TO FN
   X(0)+50
20 PRINT T;" ";
30 PRINT PEEK(T);" ";
40 IF PEEK(T)>31 THEN
   PRINT CHR$(PEEK(T)):
   GOTO 60
50 PRINT
60 NEXT T
70 DEF FN X(R)=PEEK
   23563+256*PEEK 23564
```

Running this program gives you an idea of how functions are stored in memory. Note that if no functions are being evaluated, then DEFADD contains 0.

23561 REPDEL

The number that specifies the delay before the keys repeat is held here. Any number between 0 and 255 can be POKEd into this location – 0 turns the repeat off completely, 1 gives virtually no delay and the keys start repeating straight away, while 255 slows the whole process down.

23566 TVDATA

This location is similar to K DATA with the exception that the second byte holds the horizontal character position of the last TAB or AT used.

23562 REPPLR

The repeat speed of the keys is stored here, and again can be changed to be any value between 0 and 255. 0 does not turn the repeat off, it merely makes the countdown wrap-around, ie the counter counts 0, 255, 254 etc – 1 speeds things up a lot.

23568 – 23605 STRMS

The addresses of the various channels attached to the streams are held in these locations. To start with, the first 14 bytes hold the data for streams −3 to 3. As extra streams are added, the information is inserted up to a total of 19.

23563 A DEFADD

These two locations hold the address of the user-defined function currently

23606/7 CHARS

The address of the ROM character set is held in these two locations. The address is 256 less than the first printable character, which may seem odd at first sight. If you consider that the first 31 characters are unprintable, i.e. they are control codes, then it makes sense, since the first printable character is space with a code of 32 and 32*8=256. To find the address of a character definition, the processor need only multiply the code by 8 and add this to CHARS.

A useful facility of this location is that it allows the whole character set to be reshaped. The following program relocates the character set into RAM and then redefines part of 'A' (ASCII 65).

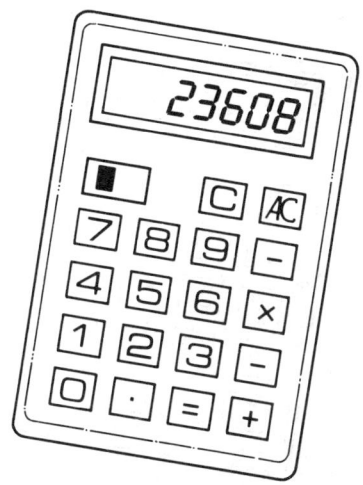

```
10  CLEAR 39999
20  PRINT "AAAAA"
30  PRINT PEEK(23606),
    PEEK(23607)
40  LET CH=PEEK(23606)+
    256*PEEK(23607)
50  LET CH=CH+256
60  FOR T=0 TO 127*8
70  POKE 40000+T,PEEK
    (15616+T)
80  NEXT T
90  POKE 23607,INT((40000-
    256)/256)
100 POKE 23606,40000-256*
    INT(40000/256)
110 REM REDEFINE PART OF 'A'
120 POKE 39744+(8*65),255
130 PRINT "AAAAA"
```

To restore the original pointer, POKE 23606,0 and POKE 23607,60

23608 RASP

The value held here specifies the length of the warning buzz.

23609 PIP

This one defines the length of the keyboard click which can be POKEd with a larger value to make the pip a little more audible.

23610 ERR NR

One less than the report code is held here and if a number is POKEd into the location, it causes the appropriate error to be generated.

23611 FLAGS

This location contains a number of flags used by the Spectrum for various operations. The eight bits are set out as follows:

Bit 1 is set (1) when stream three is to be used for output from a print command. It is zero if stream 2 is being used (3 is normally the printer and 2 is the main screen). Bit 2 is set when

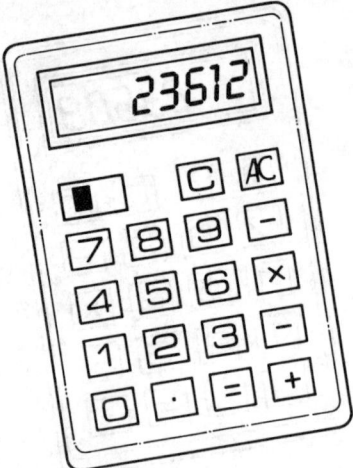

printing in 'L' mode, and zero for 'K' mode. Bit 3 is set when inputting in 'L' mode, and zero when in 'K' mode.

Bit 5 is set if a new key has been pressed since it was last set to zero.

Bit 6 is used to indicate if the current expression is a number (0) or string (1).

Bit 7 is zero when Basic is checking a line for syntax on entry and set to one when a program is being run.

Most of the flags are of little use for POKEing, but can be useful status indicators for PEEKing.

23612 TVFLAG

This set of flags is used to indicate the status of the screen.

Bit 0 is set if the lower part of the screen is being used, zero if the main screen is being handled.

Bit 3 signals that the current mode ('K', 'L' etc) may have changed and needs rechecking.

Bit 4 is set if an automatic listing is being printed. Otherwise it is zero.

Bit 5 is used to signal that the lower part of the screen needs to be cleared.

23613/4 ERR SP

The name given to this location is slightly wrong as it is actually used to point to the line where a GOSUB was called from. For instance, try:

```
10   PRINT FN A(FN A
     (23613)+2)
20   GOSUB 1000
30   STOP
100  DEF FN A(X)=PEEK X+
     256*PEEK(X+1)
1000 PRINT FN A(FN A
     (23613) +2)
1010 GOSUB 2000
1020 RETURN
2000 PRINT FN A(FN A
     (23613)+2)
2010 RETURN
```

The function FN A is used to get the 16 bit address from the location specified as its argument. Thus, if it is used twice, it gets the number pointed to by the address of the first execution. The +2 copes with the fact that the GOSUB line numbers are kept on a stack and the stack pointer has been incremented by the time we are in the subroutine. The program given above could usefully be implemented in a program that has problems with its subroutines since it tells you where each GOSUB comes from.

23617 MODE

The contents of this location define the cursor and input mode to be used. For instance, try:

```
10 INPUT"Enter a number 0-
   255 ";A
20 POKE 23617,A
```

```
30 GOTO 10
```

and notice how the different cursors appear for different numbers. Try entering numbers like 10 and 255 and note how the cursor changes to 'O' or 'I'. This can be useful when inputting data that need to be put in a certain mode, ie caps-lock or graphics.

This program can only be RUN once.

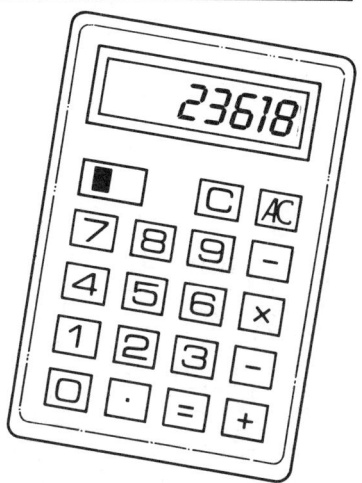

23618/9 NEWPPC
23620 NSPPC

These three can be taken together as they can be used to define the next line number and statement to be executed by Basic. For instance, try:

```
10   PRINT "LINE 10"
20   POKE 23618,1000-256*INT
     (1000/256):POKE 23619,
     INT(1000/256):
     POKE 23620,3
30   PRINT"LINE 30"
40   STOP
1000 PRINT "LINE 1000 ST1":
     PRINT"LINE 1000 ST2":
     PRINT"LINE 1000 ST3"
1010 GOTO 30
```

This program will jump directly to line 1000 statement 3, and the basic idea can be used in a number of ways, even from machine code, to jump directly into a certain Basic line.

23621/2 PPC
23623 SUBPPC

Again, these three can be taken together since they point directly to the statement currently being executed. They are not really of much use from within Basic, but they could be used from an interrupt-driven machine code routine to provide a line/statement trace facility.

23624 BORDCR

This contains the border colour multiplied by eight. Bits 6 and 7 (64 and 128) can be used to make the lower screen flash and bright. POKEing values into this location will show what happens.

23625/6 E PPC

When the LIST command is used, or an automatic listing is forced, these locations hold the number of the line that contains the editing cursor. POKEing these two locations with another line number will change it. A possible use for this is to come out of a program with the cursor in a certain position.

Alternatively, the cursor can be

removed by POKEing both of these locations with zero, useful for listings.

23627/8 VARS

The pointer to the start of the variable storage is held in these locations. This pointer may be of some use to users who want to access the Basic variable storage area from machine code programs, allowing data to be pressed back and forth without resorting to PEEKs and POKEs. The layout of the variable area is detailed in the Spectrum user guide.

23629/30 DEST

These hold the address of the first letter of the name of the variable currently in use by Basic. If this is a new variable, they point to the location immediately before E LINE, where the start of the new variable is to be stored.

23635/6 PROG

The address of the start of the Basic program is stored here. This cannot normally be altered, as on some micros, so there is no possibility of having two programs in memory at one time without altering a lot more of the pointers.

23637/8 NXTLN

The address of the next Basic line number to be executed is stored in this location. Again, there is not really much use to which this can be put, besides perhaps allowing programs to alter themselves. Try this and see what happens:

```
 10  POKE FN A(23637)+6,65
 20  REM "Hello there"
100  DEF FN A(X)=PEEK
     X+256*PEEK(X+1)
```

If you now alter line 10 to:

```
 10  POKE FN A(23637)+4,245
```

and re-run the program you'll see how programs can be made to alter themselves. A clue to what happens is that 245 is a token.

23639/40 DATADD

The address held here is used to keep track of the last data item used. If there is no more data after this statement, an 'Out of data error' occurs.

23641/2 E LINE

These two locations hold the address of the start of the editing area and point to the beginning of the line currently being edited there.

23659 DF SZ

This location contains the number of lines, including the blank one, in the lower screen (status line). This value is normally 2 but can be altered to 0 to give two more lines on the main screen. The drawback is that it must be changed back to 2 before the end of a program, otherwise the machine will crash.

The number of lines specified here can also be increased causing the scroll ? message to occur further up the screen. The problem here is that if you answer yes, you get the 'out of screen' error. So the only real use is to increase the number of screen lines to 24 like this:

```
10   LET A$=INKEY$
20   IF A$=" " THEN GOTO 100
30   POKE 23659,0:REM SEE
     SCR CT
40   PRINT"AA";
50   GOTO 10
100  POKE 23659,2
```

Note that if you break while the bottom two lines are full, the Spectrum will crash. Also don't try and use PRINT AT as this also causes a crash.

23660/1 S TOP

These two locations hold the line number where the auto list starts and POKEing these with a different number is directly equivalent to using LIST line number.

23662/3 OLDPPC

When the command CONTINUE is used, this is where the line number to restart from is kept, so running:

```
10   PRINT AT 0,0;"LINE 0"
20   STOP
100  PRINT "CONTINUE 100"
```

then POKEing 23662 with 100, and 23663 with zero, then entering CONT gives the expected result.

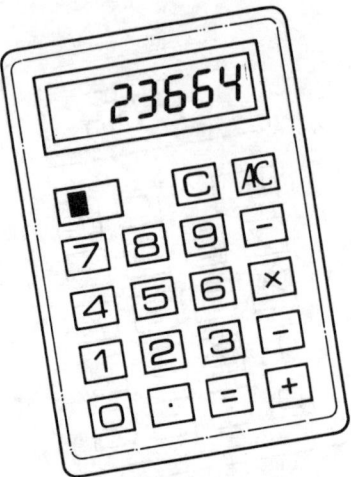

23664   OSPPC

This location can be used in the same way as OLDPPC but it points to the statement number within a line.

23670/1   SEED

The seed used to generate the random number, is stored here. POKEing numbers into this location has exactly the same effect as RANDOMIZE so:

```
10 RANDOMIZE 1
20 PRINT RND
30 POKE 23670,1:POKE
   23671,0
40 PRINT RND
```

produces the same pseudo random number.

23672   FRAMES

One of the things that the Spectrum lacks is a real time clock, or does it? FRAMES can be used to obtain fairly accurate time to an accuracy of $\frac{1}{50}$th of a second. Try:

```
10 LET T=PEEK 23672+
   (256*PEEK 23673)+
   (65536*PEEK 23674)
20 PRINT AT 0,0;INT((T/
   50)-60*INT((T/50)/60))
30 GOTO 10
```

to get seconds. Since the number of frames sent to the screen is counted in 3 bytes, the max number of $\frac{1}{50}$ths of a second in 24 hours is:
16777216, and the number of $\frac{1}{50}$ths of a second in 24 hours is:
4320000. This means that there is ample room for a 24 hour clock. Simply work out the correct numbers and POKE them into FRAMES. A subroutine similar to the seconds demo above will then provide the current time.

23675/6   UDG

As with the character set pointer CHARS, UDG points to the user defined graphics. There are a number of uses to which this pointer can be put. First it can be altered to point higher up in memory, leaving some space for a machine code routine. Alternatively, it could be used to point to a number of different character sets defined in RAM. This is a little easier than altering the standard character set, as USR "A" always returns the address of the UDG set pointed to by 23675/6, so the same routines can be used to define all the different UDG sets. Switching between them is simply a matter of changing this pointer.

23677/8 COORDS

The horizontal and vertical coordinates of the last point PLOTted are held here. This also applies to the DRAW command and so these locations can be used to provide an absolute move command that allows the PLOT position to be relocated without having to resort to INVERSE. Try

```
10 PLOT 0,0
20 DRAW 10,10
30 POKE 23677,50
40 POKE 23678,60
50 DRAW 10,10
```

23684 DF CC

These locations hold the address of the print position in the display file and could be used to provide an alternative print routine.

23686/7 DFCCL

Of more use are locations 23686/7 as they normally give the address of the start of the lower screen. This address can be used along with a few others discussed earlier to provide a routine for printing messages on the lower screen. This program does just this using the pointer to CHARS to get the information about the character shapes.

```
10 BORDER 0
20 DIM A$(31)
30 LET LS=FN A(23686)
40 INPUT A$
50 FOR T=1 TO LEN (A$)
```

```
60   FOR S=0 TO 7
70   POKE LS-1+(S*256)+T,
     PEEK((CODE (A$(T TO
     T)))*8+FN A(23606)+S)
80   NEXT S
90   NEXT T
100  PRINT"USE BREAK TO GET
     OUT OF THE PROGRAM"
110  GOTO 100
1000 DEF FN A(X)=PEEK
     X+256*PEEK(X+1)
```

Note that exactly the same routine can be used to print on the main screen simply by setting LS to 16384 in line 30.

23688/9 S POSN

The screen print position is held here. Oddly enough it takes its origin as the bottom left hand corner of the screen so the normal PRINT AT 0,0;"a" will cause these two locations to hold 33 and 22 and not 0,0. They can be POKEd to provide a kind of PRINT AT but this is likely to cause a crash.

23692 SCR CT

This location is used by the system to control the scrolling of the screen and when it reaches 1 the 'Scroll?' message is displayed. This can be avoided by POKEing a 0 or 2 into it before each print statement. This can be used to make the routine used to increase the screen size (see DF SZ) a little safer; simply add 35 POKE 23692,0 to get rid of the temptation to break into the program.

As you can see, quite a few of the system variables can be of some use and, although there are times when care should be taken, don't be afraid to experiment a little as there is always the option of pulling the plug when the Spectrum crashes. Tailoring of the character set and printing at unusual places on the screen can come in very useful in your own programs and, if you ever become a machine code 'freak', you'll probably find some of the more obscure system variables provide the chance to do something really slick, which, after all, is the joy of programming.

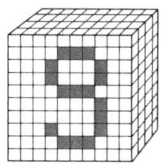

User-defined graphics

Up to a point it's very easy to understand how the Spectrum's user-defined graphics operate, as it's simply a question of assigning eight binary numbers to an 8×8 grid matrix that makes up one user-defined character, for example:

```
10 POKE USR "A"+0, BIN
   10101010
20 POKE USR "A"+1, BIN
   01010101
30 POKE USR "A"+2, BIN
   10101010
40 POKE USR "A"+3, BIN
   01010101
50 POKE USR "A"+4, BIN
   10101010
60 POKE USR "A"+5, BIN
   01010101
70 POKE USR "A"+6, BIN
   10101010
80 POKE USR "A"+7, BIN
   01010101
90 PRINT "A": REM UDG
```

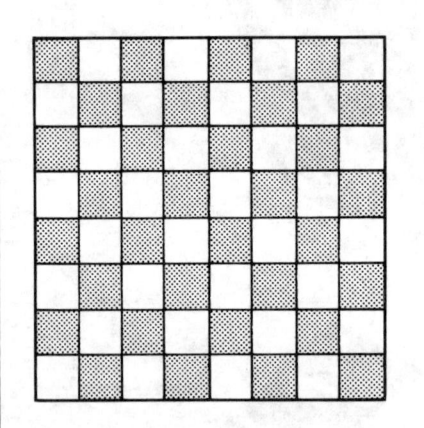

The eight lines above will POKE a hatchwork pattern into the Spectrum's graphic 'A', and you can see the sort of pattern that will develop from the 1s and 0s in the binary numbers. Clearly as you're specifying BIN before the number – try it without and the Spectrum will assume it's decimal, and give you an 'integer out of range' message – you can ease the typing problems by converting the number to decimal. You can also POKE the numbers in from DATA statements, using a FOR...NEXT loop;

```
10 FOR N=0 TO 7: READ B:
   POKE USR "A"+N,B: NEXT N
20 DATA 170,85,170,85,170,
   85,170,85
```

Now if you're sharp-eyed you'll have noticed something significant about the decimal numbers that isn't immediately obvious from the binary version, and that is that every second number is half the one before. You'll see why by looking at the binary version, where they've had the zero on the end lopped off. The reason for this is that dividing a binary number by two is just like dividing a decimal number by ten.

This becomes even clearer if you try this:

```
10 FOR N=0 TO 7: POKE USR
   "A"+N,INT(255/(2↑N)):
   NEXT N
```

By repeatedly dividing by two and INTing it you're producing the series of numbers 255,127,63,31,15,7,3,1, forming a sort of wedge shape.

You should now be beginning to see how arithmetical operations can be used with UDGs. Performing calculations on the numbers the UDG locations contain can be important for animation – we'll explore that later, but can you guess how it's done now?

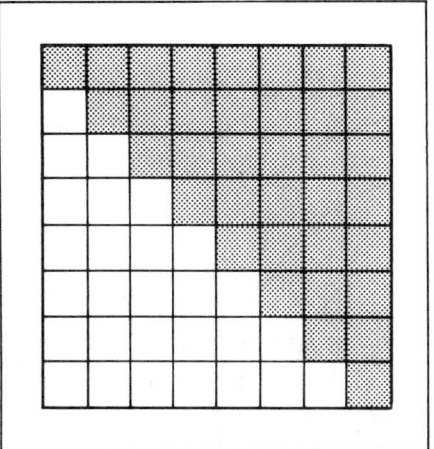

Graphics and memory

```
20 FOR I=0 TO 7
30 POKE 65368+I,INT
   (RND*256)
40 NEXT I
50 PRINT AT 10,16;"A":
   REM UDG
60 NEXT N
```

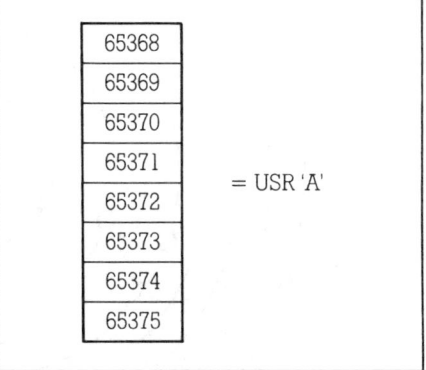

The difficulty many Spectrum users face when they're dealing with user-defined graphics is one of coming to terms with what's actually going on when you program them. In this sense UDGs are their own worst enemy, because they're so easy to program that you're liable to miss the opportunity to learn more about how the Spectrum's memory operates.

What you should understand is that the Spectrum's UDG area of memory is really just another stack of memory locations. For example:

PRINT USR "A"

This prints the location of the first of the eight addresses that make up the Spectrum's graphic A, 65368, so the expression USR 'A' is just a way of avoiding having to remember a specific memory location.

Try this:

```
10 FOR N=1 TO 10
```

This little program redefines graphic A by POKEing random numbers into it, and cycles through this ten times – try going into graphics and typing A to confirm that 65368 is just the same as USR 'A'. A short routine like this is easily incorporated in a game, but there are more systematic ways of handling UDGs:

```
 5 LET P=167
10 FOR N=0 TO 167
20 POKE USR "A"+N,PEEK
   (15880+P)
30 LET P=P-1
40 NEXT N
```

This is simply a loop that counts through N and P, so that when N is 0 P is 167, down to N being 167 and P being 0. In line 20 we're POKEing into the 168 locations (21 user-defined graphics times 8 locations). Now the first address of the Spectrum's character A in ROM is 15880, and as these are organised on exactly the

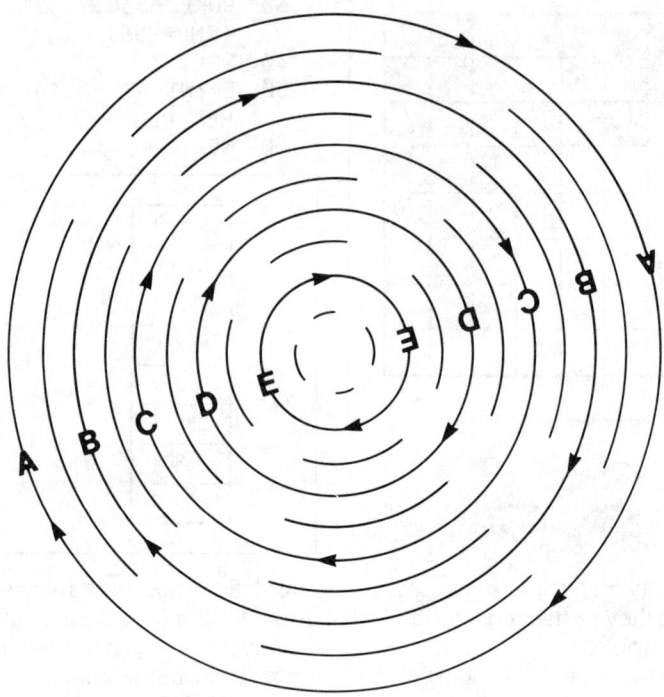

same basis as the user-defined graphics character set, 15880 plus 167 gives you the last address of the character U. So we're PEEKing backwards from there, and POKEing forward into the UDG set, leaving us with an inverted and backward character set!

If we'd performed this operation on the UDG set, incidentally, we'd have found the first half of the UDG character set was a mirror image of the second half.

But with what we have above you don't actually get a complete character set. Just to show there's very little real difference between UDG memory and other areas of memory, try this one:

```
10  CLEAR 59999
20  FOR N=0 TO 1024
30  POKE 60000+N,PEEK
    (15360+N)
40  NEXT N
50  POKE 23607,234
60  POKE 23606,96
```

Run this and, provided you've typed it in right, you'll see no difference at all. Those of you who can see a real and unpleasant difference (your character set is corrupted) should type:

```
POKE 23606,0:POKE 23607,60
```

and check your listing again. What we're doing here is reserving space above 59999 for a complete copy of the Spectrum's character set. Line 30 copies the dot patterns from 15360 on into the locations from 60000 on.

Now the important lines are 50 and 60, which alter the address of the system variable CHARS, which keeps track of where the Spectrum looks to find its character set. As the address of the character set is clearly going to be larger than 255, the largest number you can have in one location, it clearly needs two locations. You calculate CHARS like this:

```
PRINT PEEK 23606+256*PEEK 23607
```

Working backwards from this, as we want to point CHARS at 60000 (we could put it anywhere else, within reason) we divide 60000 by 256, giving us 234.375, so the number in 23607 must be 234. Then multiply 234 by 256, take that away from 60000 and it gives us 96, which is the number to go into 23606.

Now to show you one way to use this, add these lines:

```
60  FOR N=96 TO 120
70  POKE 23606,N
80  LIST
90  NEXT N
100 POKE 23606,96
```

When we said the character set was corrupted, that wasn't strictly true. The lines we've added here are simply shifting the pointer to the character set one address at a time, so with each successive pass through the second loop the character set is shifting upwards, so that eventually it becomes totally unintelligible.

You could use this as a security method, but you can make listings just as unreadable by POKEing odd numbers into 23606 and 23607 without moving the character set at all.

User-defined graphics

Adding character

Using the method above you can see it would be quite easy to get the Spectrum to use an alternative character set, but you'd still have to sit down with graph paper and draw up your character set. Or would you?

In fact, you wouldn't. Unless you're talking about Chinese or Arabic, character sets usually have quite a lot in common – logically enough, because if they didn't you wouldn't be able to read them. So if you think about what you want to do it's often possible to perform a systematic operation on the character set that will result in a new typeface at the cost of very little typing.

TRY THIS

Consider the problem of producing an italic face. This is essentially a typeface that slopes, so by moving the top rows of the character's dot pattern to one side, and the bottom rows to the other, you could produce a fair simulation of italics:

```
20   CLEAR 64529
30   FOR T=32 TO 127
40   FOR S=0 TO 8
50   LET A=PEEK(15360+
     (T*8)+S)
60   IF S>=0 AND S<4 THEN
     LET A=A/2
70   IF S=6 OR S=7 THEN
     LET A=A*2
80   LET A=A-((A>255)*256)
90   POKE 64273+(T*8)+S,A
100  NEXT S
110  NEXT T
120  GOSUB 1000
140  PRINT "THIS IS WHAT ";
150  GOSUB 2000
160  PRINT "ITALICS ":GOSUB
     1000: PRINT "LOOK
     LIKE. ": GOSUB 2000:
     PRINT "OK!"
170  FOR T=0 TO 5
180  GOSUB 1000:PRINT
     "ABCDEFGHIJKLM"
190  GOSUB 2000:
     PRINT"ABCDEFGHIJKLM"
200  NEXT T
210  STOP
1000 POKE 23606,0: POKE
     23607,60
1010 RETURN
2000 POKE 23606,64273-256*
     INT(64273/256)
2010 POKE 23607,INT(64273/
     256)
2020 RETURN
```

It should be fairly easy for you to work out what's going on here. Address 15360 in line 50 is the start of the character set, but the part we're really interested in begins a little further on. I can't visualise what an italic space looks like either, but we'll let that pass!

Line 60 uses S to check to see if we're on the top four pixel lines of the dot pattern, and if so shifts them one pixel to the right by dividing the number by two. The fifth and sixth lines are left as they are, and the seventh and eighth lines are multiplied by two, shifting them one to the left.

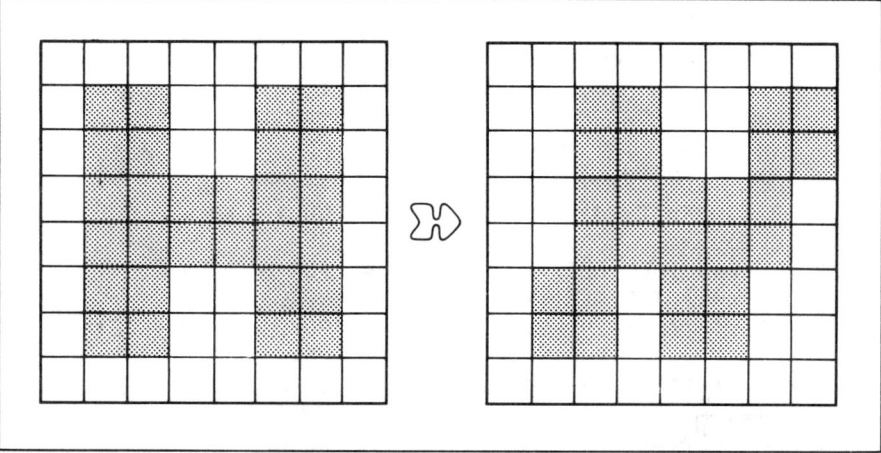

Line 80 checks to see if the resulting number is too big to fit in an address, and if so lops off 256.

And, apart from POKEing the new set in at line 90, that's it. The rest of the program gives you a demonstration of what the set looks like, and the subroutines at 1000 and 2000 respectively switch the character set between the normal one and the italic one. The program takes a while to produce results.

UDGs and the screen

If you construct your programs from user-defined graphics alone you're really missing out on something. Certainly it's easy to build the screens for programs out of user-defined blocks, but the Spectrum has other facilities that you can take advantage of. By messing around with the scrolling, for example, you can produce interesting effects easily.

TRY THIS

As you know the Spectrum's screen is organised in rather a complex way, so manipulating it can be difficult. The following program, however, incorporates two machine code routines that will scroll the top and bottom thirds of the screen. It's been organised that way to allow you to use the routines singly if you wish:

```
10 CLEAR 59999
20 GOSUB 500
30 LET X=10: LET Z=16
40 FOR N=60000 TO 60033
50 READ E
```

```
 60 POKE N,E
 70 NEXT N
100 LET Y=40: LET YY=120
110 LET D=INT (RND*2): LET
    PP=(1 AND D=1)+(-1
    AND D=0)
120 LET C=INT (RND*2): LET
    P=(1 AND C=1)+(-1 AND
    C=0)
130 IF Y=0 THEN LET P=1
140 IF Y=40 THEN LET P=-1
150 IF YY=174 THEN LET
    PP=-1
160 IF YY=115 THEN LET
    PP=1
170 LET Y=Y+P: LET
    YY=YY+PP
180 PLOT 0,Y: DRAW 0,-Y:
    PLOT 0,YY: DRAW
    0,175-YY
190 PRINT AT X,Z;" "
200 IF INKEY$="1" THEN LET
    X=X-1
210 IF INKEY$="q" THEN LET
    X=X+1
220 PRINT AT X,Z;"A":
    REM UDG
230 LET B=USR 60000: LET
    A=USR 60017
240 GO TO 110
499 REM SET UP UDG
500 FOR N=0 TO 7
510 READ E
520 POKE USR "A"+N,E
530 NEXT N
540 DATA 7,30,124,255,124,
    30,7,0
550 RETURN
680 DATA 33,0,80,62,63,6,
    32,183,203,30,35,16,
    251,61,32,245,201
690 DATA 33,0,64,62,63,6,
    32,183,203,30,35,16,
    251,61,32,245,201
```

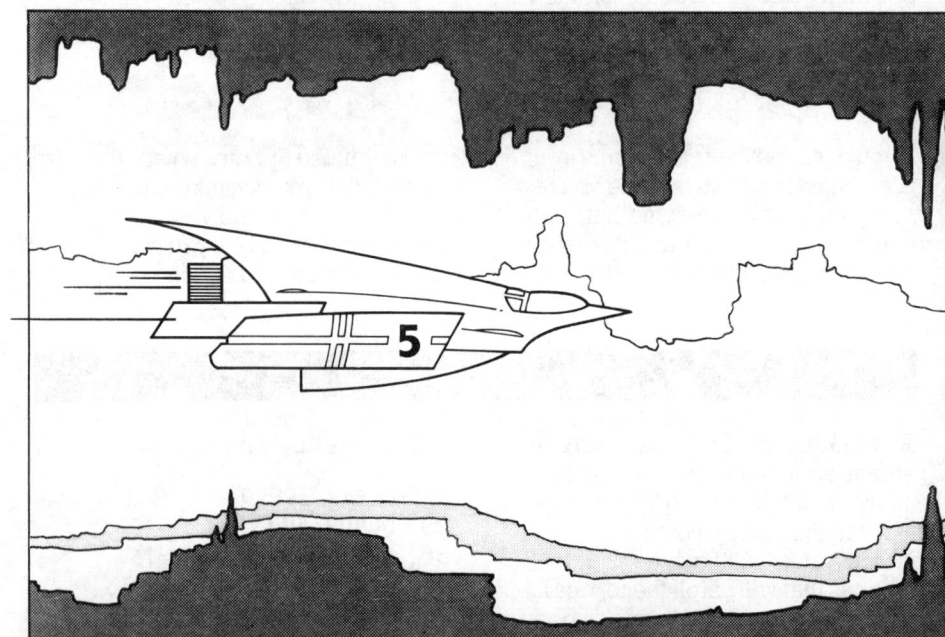

The crucial elements of this program are in lines 680 and 690. These are basically the same routine except for the third piece of data, which governs the screen address the routine starts from. In the case of the first routine the number is 680, and if you use the same method we used to deal with CHARS i.e. multiply it by 256 and add the number in the address before it, we get 20480, which is the start address of the bottom third of the screen. The same operation performed on the routine in line 690 gives us 16384, the start address of the top third of the screen.

From this you'll see what we're doing is scrolling the top and the bottom of the screen independently, leaving your UDG spaceship in the centre. We're using PLOT and DRAW to generate the scenery, which slows it up somewhat, but you could speed it up a little by not filling in the scenery, and you could add a routine check to see if you'd hit the cave walls. This would just involve making sure the ATTRibutes of X,Z equalled a space before you printed the ship on it.

Should you wish to pull the scrolling routines out for use in other games, you'll find the top part is called by LET B=USR 60000 and the bottom part by LET A=USR 60017. You could also use RANDOMIZE USR instead of LET A=USR, as it's just a matter of locking the Spectrum into the relevant routine at regular intervals.

Checklist

In this chapter you should have learned:

☐ How USR 'A' etc is just shorthand for one of the Spectrum's memory locations, and how dot patterns are stored in the UDG area.

☐ How to manipulate the shape of a character on the screen by performing arithmetical operations on the number stored in memory.

☐ How to page in completely new character sets by varying the value stored in system variable CHARS, producing just about as many user-defined graphics as you're ever likely to want.

☐ How to use scrolling routines mixed with UDGs to produce simple games.

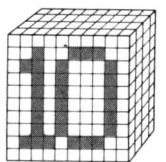

Sprites and animation

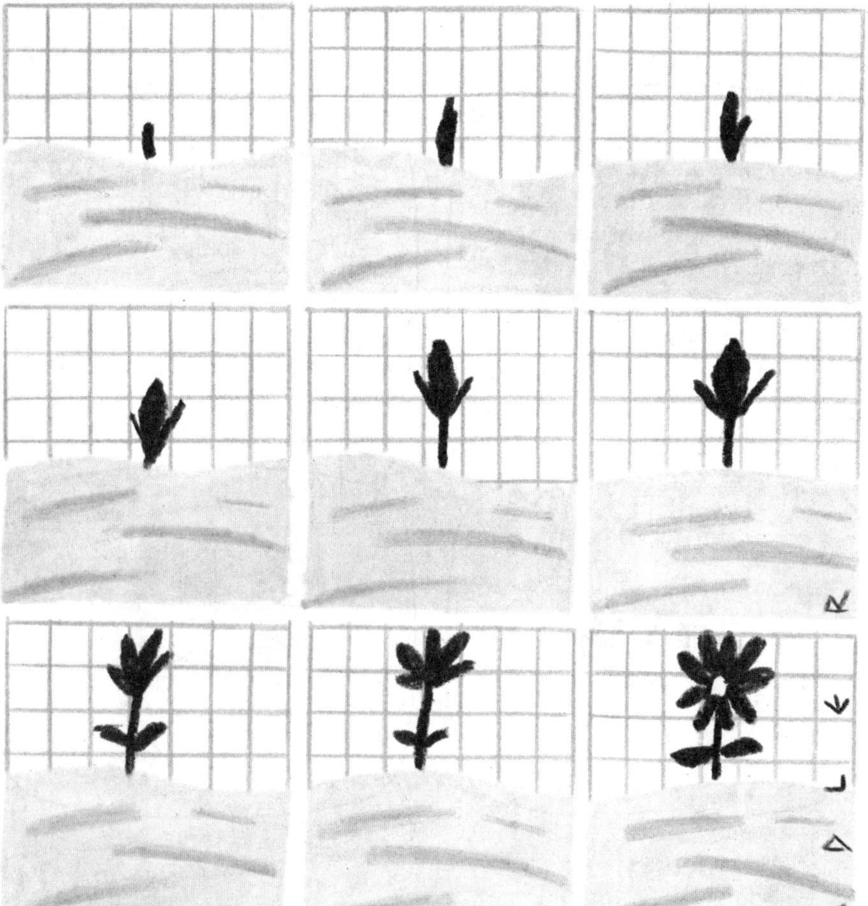

Animation is basically a way to make pictures move on the screen. There are various levels at which this can be done, the simplest being to have a Basic routine that prints a character onto the screen, rubs it out, and then prints it at the next position like this:

```
10  PRINT AT 10,0;"M";
20  FOR T=0 TO 30
30  PRINT AT 10,T;" ";
40  PRINT AT 10,T+1;"M";
50  NEXT T
60  FOR T=31 TO 0 STEP -1
70  PRINT AT 10,T;" ";
80  PRINT AT 10,T-1;"M"
90  NEXT T
100 GOTO 10
```

After typing in this program, you should have an 'M' whizzing back and forth across the screen. The problem with this approach is, as you will have noticed, that it is jerky, and it flickers a lot. The general idea, however, is the basis for sprites and movement of any single figure.

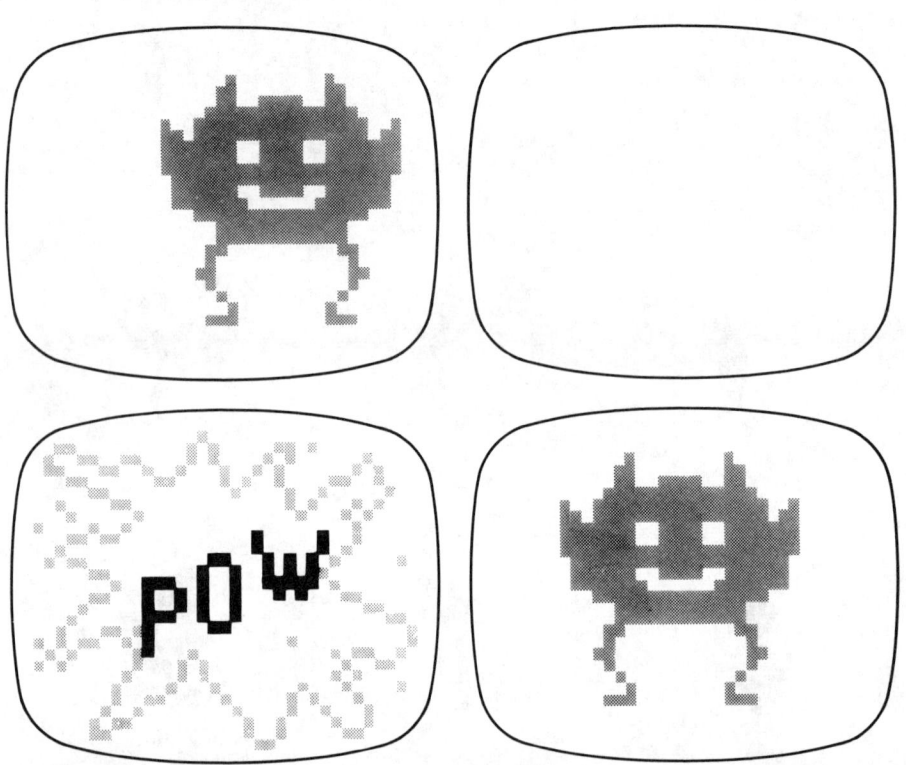

Screen layout

To get an idea of how sprites actually work, we'll have a quick overview of how the Spectrum's screen works.

The picture is made up from a series of horizontal lines, each of which is again split into a number of dots. These lines and dots give the resolution of the screen in pixels. The Spectrum's screen, as with a number of other micros, is also split into two main sections, the border and the main screen. As the screen is drawn, at 50 times a second, the television's scanning beam is effectively turned on and off depending on its position and the contents of the video RAM. The hardware that is responsible for doing all of the screen data handling is the famous Sinclair ULA.

During the first part of the scan, this just sends out a single colour signal that forms the top part of the border. As soon as the printable section of the screen is reached, the ULA first sends out the border signal and then scans the video RAM and, if a bit contains a one, a dot is sent out; if it's a zero, then a space is sent. After the picture line has been drawn, the ULA resumes drawing the border until the lower border is reached, when it just sends out a single colour.

As well as scanning the picture part of the RAM, from 16384 to 22528, the ULA also scans the attribute section, from 22528 to 23296, to form the colours on the screen. The colour signals cause the picture information to be sent to the different colour guns in the TV and, if you have a colour television, this creates a pretty colour picture.

When you move characters around the screen, a lot of the flickering is caused by interference between the screen scan and writing into the screen RAM. Since the object has to be erased and then re-drawn to make it move, the ULA scan will probably pick up the picture halfway through either the erase part of the program, or somewhere in the re-draw section, giving rise to severe ghosting and flickering, and generally making quite a mess of things.

Fortunately, all is not lost, as there are times when the ULA is not actually scanning the video RAM, e.g. when it is drawing the border, or when the beam is 'flying back' to the top of the picture. These times are when all the redrawing should be done.

To get back to sprites, the following section describes a set of machine code routines that allow you to place characters anywhere on the screen (at any of 0–255, 0–175 horizontal, vertical positions).

The following program is used to load the sprite machine code into memory and then store it on either microdrive or tape.

```
10  REM LOADER PROGRAM FOR
    SPRITES
20  FOR T=30022 TO 30176
30  READ A:POKE T,A
40  NEXT T
50  SAVE *"M";1;"SPRT.BIN"
    CODE 30000,175
60  STOP
100 DATA 205,129,117,205,
    119,117,201,205,170
110 DATA 117,201,42,68,117,1,
    56,117,22,8,126,2
120 DATA 3,35,21,32,249,201,
    205,170,117
```

```
130 DATA 58,66,117,50,64,
    117,58,67,117,50,65
140 DATA 117,205,129,117,
    205,119,117,201,205
150 DATA 81,117,33,56,117,
    205,173,117,201,33
160 DATA 48,117,237,75,64,
    117,22,8,30,8
170 DATA 197,213,229,205,
    206,34,205,213,45
180 DATA 225,209,193,203,
    47,203,22,12,29
190 DATA 32,236,35,5,121,
    214,8,79,21,32
200 DATA 225,201,33,48,117,
    237,75,64,117
210 DATA 22,8,30,8,203,38,
    218,191
220 DATA 117,62,12,50,145,
    92,197,213,229
230 DATA 205,229,34,225,
    209,193,62,0,50
240 DATA 145,92,12,29,32,
    228,121,214,8,79
250 DATA 35,5,21,194,179,
    117,201
260 DATA 80,11,114,99,101
```

This machine code allows any character to be moved around the screen as a sprite. Before the sprite is moved to a particular position on the screen, the data at that position is stored. After the sprite has moved on, this data is replaced so that the background does not get messed up by any sprite movements.

To use the program, the following addresses need to be noted:

30020 (ADL) holds the low byte of the address of the character to be used as the sprite.

30021 (ADH) holds the high byte of the address.

30016 (X) holds the start horizontal position of the sprite.

30017 (Y) holds the start vertical position of the sprite.

30018 (X1) holds the horizontal position of the coordinate to which the sprite is to be moved with MSPR.

30019 (Y1) holds the vertical position to be moved to.

30022 (SPON) Executing at this address turns the sprite on.

30029 (SPOF) This one turns the sprite off.

30049 (MSPR) This moves the sprite from X,Y to X1,Y1 and after it has finished X becomes X1, Y becomes Y1.

With this information, you have everything you need to be able to shift the sprite around the screen. Note that since the position specified by X and Y is a pixel position, the character can be placed anywhere on the screen.

Here is a demonstration:

```
10  GOSUB 1000:REM LOAD
    MACHINE CODE
20  LET X=30016
30  LET Y=30017
40  LET X1=30018
50  LET Y1=30019
60  LET CL=30020
70  LET CH=30021
80  LET SPON=30022
90  LET SPOF=30029
100 LET MSPR=30049
110 LET DX=1:LET DY=1
120 LET SX=10:LET SY=10
130 POKE CH,255:POKE CL,88
140 POKE X,SX:POKE Y,SY
150 RANDOMIZE USR SPON
160 LET SX=SX+DX:LET
    SY=SY+DY
170 IF SX>240 OR SX<10
    THEN LET DX=-DX
180 IF SY>160 OR SY<10
    THEN LET DY=-DY
190 POKE X1,SX:POKE Y1,SY
200 RANDOMIZE USR MSPR
```

```
 210  GOTO 160
1000  LOAD *"M";1;"SPRT.
      BIN"CODE
1010  RETURN
```

Just to prove that the background will not be erased, add the following line:

```
 105  FOR T=0 TO 600:
      PRINT"B";:NEXT T
```

The other use for the sprite routines is to allow printing anywhere on the screen so try the following:

```
 10  GOSUB 1000:REM LOAD
     MACHINE CODE
 20  LET X=30016: LET Y=
     30017: LET X1=30018:
     LET Y1=30019: LET
     CL=30020: LET CH=30021:
     LET SPON=30022: LET
     LET SPOF=30029: LET
     MSPR=30049
110  FOR T=65 TO 85
120  POKE CL,(USR
     CHR$(T))—
     256*INT(USR CHR$(T)/
     256)
130  POKE CH,INT(USR
     CHR$(T)/256)
140  POKE X,FN R(200)+10
150  POKE Y,FN R(100)+10
160  RANDOMIZE USR SPON
170  NEXT T
180  DEF FN R(X)=
     INT(RND*X)-1
999  STOP
1000 LOAD*"M";1;"SPRT.
     BIN" CODE
1010 RETURN
```

By altering the address poked into CH and CL to point to the character ROM, found by adding the CODE of the character to:

(33*8)+256+PEEK(23606)+256*PEEK(23607)

you can display any of the printable characters anywhere.

Full screen animation

Another type of animation is that used in cartoons, consisting of a sequence of snapshots of a figure in a set of positions each of which is slightly moved on from the previous one. On the Spectrum this can be achieved by drawing the first snapshot onto the screen and saving the whole screen into memory. The next shot is then drawn, and the next, and the next.

All of the screens are saved into memory as a series that can be loaded to the video RAM in sequence. There are two main drawbacks to doing this, the first being the amount of memory that each screen takes up (about 6K). The second drawback is that from Basic, it would take an appreciable amount of time to transfer the data.

Fortunately, the speed at which this can be done can be increased dramatically by using a machine code routine. The Z80 microprocessor at the heart of the Spectrum has a special command for copying sections of memory around at high speed, so the routine to copy the screens around is nice and short.

If you try the following program, you will see that images can be swapped from screen to memory pretty quickly.

```
 10  CLEAR 50000
 20  LET SWAP=50000
 30  GOSUB 200
```

```
40  FOR T=0 TO 255 STEP 5
50  PLOT 0,0
60  DRAW T,175
70  NEXT T
80  RANDOMIZE USR SWAP
90  CLS
100 FOR T=-255 TO 0 STEP 5
110 PLOT 255,0
120 DRAW T,175
130 NEXT T
140 RANDOMIZE USR SWAP
150 GOTO 140
200 FOR T=SWAP TO SWAP+29
210 READ A:POKE T,A
220 NEXT T
230 RETURN
240 DATA 33,0,64,17,0,224,
    1,0
250 DATA 27,126,245,26,119,
    241,18,11
260 DATA 35,19,120,177,32,
    243,177,32
270 DATA 243,201,107,101,
    110,110
```

The first screen is drawn and then swapped into memory, with RANDOMIZE USR SWAP, which happens to be empty. The next picture is then drawn and the two swapped over.

A thing to note is that the routine is relocatable, i.e. it can be placed anywhere in RAM simply by altering the value of SWAP. You should, however remember to change the CLEAR statement. But, it is not the fastest way of doing things and, as you can see, it flickers.

A much better method is to use the following suite of programs to store the images in memory and then recall them in sequence to the screen.

The first program loads the machine code from a series of data statements and then saves the appropriate section of memory to tape or microdrive. It is reloaded later on using:

```
LOAD *"M";1;"TRN.BIN"
CODE 65280
```

or for tape:

```
LOAD "TRN.BIN" CODE 65280
```

This machine code is used to copy a section of memory whose address must be put into addresses 65280 and 65281. The first holds the low byte of the address, obtained from:

```
LO.ADDR=ADDR-256*INT(ADDR/256)
```

The location, 65281, holds the high byte of the address, found by:

```
HI.ADDR=INT(ADDR/256)
```

Once these two numbers have been entered, the machine code program knows where the screen data is to be moved from and, using RANDOMIZE USR 65282, executes the code, moving that portion of memory to the screen. Note that the attribute memory is not used, allowing the routine to work that little bit faster.

Loader program for animation.

```
 9 REM LOAD THE MACHINE
   CODE, AND SAVE AS
   TRN.BIN THIS IS USED TO
   TRANSFER MEMORY TO
   SCREEN.
10 FOR T=65280 TO 65295
20 READ A:POKE T,A
30 NEXT T
40 SAVE *"M";1;"TRN.BIN"
   CODE 65280,15
50 DATA 192,165,42,0,255,17,
   0,64,1,0
60 DATA 24,237,176,201,80,
   11,114,99,101
```

The next program demonstrates how each part of the animation is formed and copied into memory. There is room in memory for a maximum of about five to six pictures, depending upon the length of the program used to draw them. This program does take quite a long time to copy the screen from one point to another, and demonstrates the amazing speed of Z80 machine code in comparison to Basic. The copying can be done in machine code with a very similar routine to that used to call up the pictures:

```
ORG 65280
start DEFW 0        :Set aside
```
some memory space for the address to be moved to.

LD HL,16384 :Put the screen address into the HL registers.

LD DE,(start) :Load the DE registers with the address of the memory location to be moved to.

LD BC,6144 :Load BC with the length of the screen 6144 bytes.

LDIR : This is the instruction that performs the trick of copying the memory all in one go, using the HL, DE and BC registers.

RET : Return to Basic

Don't worry too much if you don't understand any of this. All you really need to know is how to use it and the numbers of the assembled code.

To use it, just replace the subroutine in the design program opposite, starting at line 100, with:

```
100 LET AD=30000+(S*6192)
110 POKE 65280,AD-256*
    INT(AD/256)
120 POKE 65281,INT(AD/256)
130 RANDOMIZE USR 65282
140 RETURN
```

and add the following lines to it.

```
  5 GOSUB 200
200 FOR T=65280 TO 65295
210 READ A:POKE T,A
220 NEXT T
230 RETURN
240 DATA 0,0,33,0,64,237,
    91,0,255,1,0
250 DATA 24,237,176,201,74,
    111,104,110
```

This now does the whole thing a great deal faster.

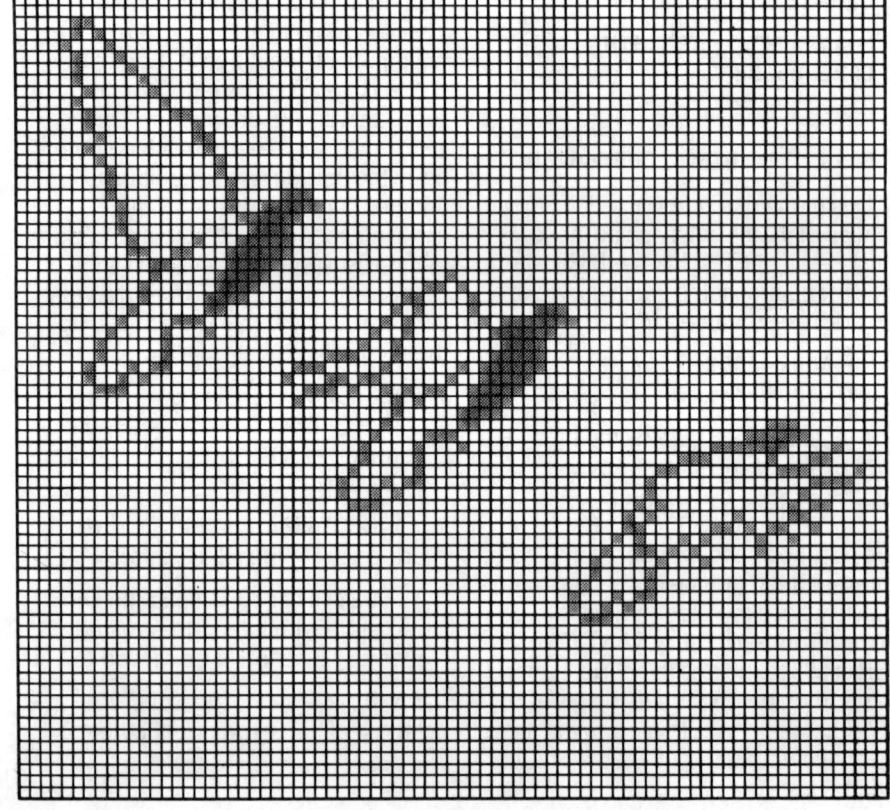

Design program

```
10  FOR T=10 TO 50 STEP 10
15  LET S=(T/10)-1
20  CLS
30  CIRCLE 100,100,T:
    CIRCLE 150,90,T/3:
    CIRCLE 140,110,T/2
40  PRINT"SCREEN NO. ";S:
    PAUSE 100
50  GOSUB 100
60  NEXT T
70  SAVE *"M";1;"RAIN" CODE
    30000,35280
80  STOP
99  REM READ SCREEN DATA
    INTO MEMORY
100 FOR D=0 TO 6144
110 POKE 30000+D+(6192*S),
    PEEK(16384+D)
120 NEXT D
130 RETURN
```

The next thing to be done is to animate the screens. This means loading to the main screen RAM with the picture data in sequence, using the machine code routine loaded and saved previously.

```
10  CLEAR 30000
20  GOSUB 100
30  FOR T=30000 TO
    30000+(4*6192) STEP
    6192
40  POKE 65280,T-256*
    INT(T/256)
50  POKE 65281,INT(T/256)
60  RANDOMIZE USR 65282
70  NEXT T
80  GOTO 30
99  REM LOAD MACHINE CODE
    AND SCREEN DATA
100 PRINT "LOADING CODE"
105 LOAD*"M";1;"TRN.BIN"
    CODE 65280
110 LOAD*"M";1;"RAIN" CODE
    30000
120 RETURN
```

Once you have run this, you should be able to work out why the picture file is called 'RAIN'.

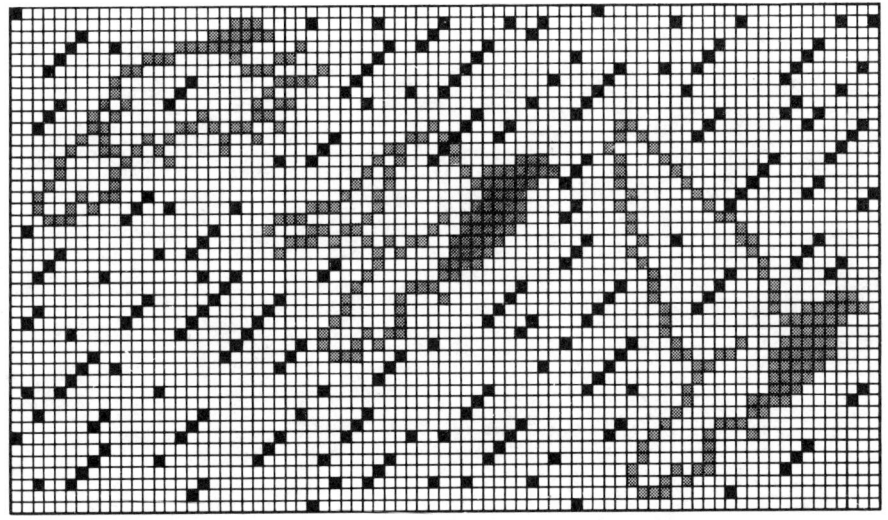

Projects

- [ ] Try setting up a more detailed full screen animation sequence.

- [ ] Alter the Basic part of the sprite routine to allow more than one sprite to be used.

- [ ] Change the full screen animation programs to include the attribute RAM for full colour.

- [ ] Incorporate the full screen animation method into the adventure program described in chapter 3 to allow pictures of the locations to be shown instead of just descriptions.

- [ ] See if you can encode the screen data used in full screen animation to allow more screens to be used. Note that a great deal of the data in each picture is the same.

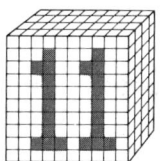

Memory in detail

Every now and again in this book you'll have run into areas where you've been told 'you don't really need to understand this right now'. Quite often this will have referred to a stack of numbers held in DATA statements that, when you POKE them into memory, seem to do incredible things, and do them a lot faster than Basic does.

You'll probably have also seen the same thing in magazines, and here you'll usually only be told it's a 'machine code program'; if you want to know more about machine code this isn't really very helpful. Clearly these numbers mean something, but what?

To get a grasp of this you really have to take a step back and think of what the Spectrum actually is, and how its memory is structured. In essence, it's a series of switches that can be either on or off, and these switches interact with one another to store numbers. The Spectrum doesn't actually store anything but numbers, so when it's 'storing' text, graphics and so on it's actually a numeric representation of whatever you think it's storing.

Therefore, whenever you type in a Basic command the Spectrum's Basic interpreter has to translate the command before the machine can act on it, and it acts on it by turning that command into a number, or a series of numbers, then executing it. In essence this is why Basic is slow compared to machine code.

What you're doing with the DATA statements of decimal numbers is talking to the Spectrum in the language it understands, and the numbers in these statements are actually a series of commands, forming

a machine code program. You've already learned that machine code should be stored above RAMtop, and therefore you should lower RAMtop to provide enough space to hold your programs (all you need do is lower it by the number of DATA statements you have), and that you execute the machine code with the call RANDOMIZE USR (address), where address is the first address of the program, ie the first location above the new RAMtop.

Why RANDOMIZE USR? It's common for micros to have an EXEC or CALL command for running machine code, and it's fairly obvious from the command what this does. It's less so in the case of the Spectrum, but once you've grasped it it's also pretty clear.

If you check with the manual you'll find RANDOMIZE is used as a pointer, and by adding USR you're telling the Spectrum you wish to point at a memory address. The Spectrum then jumps to that address, reads your first command and you're off.

Assembler

Even if you manage to master your hex times tables you'll have a communications problem. You'll still be faced with the problem of thinking in English and trying to communicate directly with something that thinks in numbers. This is basically what an assembler is all about. An assembler is a program that uses easily remembered mnemonics for you to type in, and communicates with the computer in the numbers it understands. Note however that there is a fundamental difference between an assembler and the Basic language.

In the case of Basic you're giving the computer a series of instructions that it stores, then interprets one at a time, whereas in assembler you're still POKEing the information directly into memory, even though it doesn't always feel like that's what you're doing. It's no part of this book's function to explain machine code or assembler, but it's important that you understand what they are, if only for future reference.

Hexplanation time

Don't panic if you still reckon the numbers are meaningless, because broadly speaking you're right. Because computers think in terms of binary switches, although they understand decimal numbers as instructions they're not organised in a particularly logical way. However, if you were to translate those numbers into hexadecimal, i.e. base 16, you'd start to see some sort of system behind them.

TRY THIS

Sound is a good example of what you can do in machine code by addressing the Spectrum's memory directly. If you've experimented with the sound facilities of the Spectrum you'll probably be acutely disappointed, particularly if you've had a chance to hear what other machines can produce.

The most important problem with the Spectrum's sound is the fact that all its operations are controlled by its Z80 processor. This means that sound is just one of the other operations, whereas on many other micros it is controlled by a separate processor, and the end result is that, when you're programming in Basic, everything else stops while the Spectrum BEEPs.

In machine code, however, you can get around this. You can use interrupts to produce noise while the program is apparently still executing – although in fact it's stopping very briefly at regular intervals, and you can also produce versions of the sort of sounds you'd more normally associate with arcade games, like this:

```
10  CLEAR 65205
20  FOR X=65206 TO 65280
30  READ A
40  POKE X,A
50  NEXT X
60  DATA 58,72,92,31,31,31,
    230,7,14,255
70  DATA 38,0,68,203,231,
    211,254,16,254,68
80  DATA 203,167,211,254,16,
    254,203,231,211,254
90  DATA 16,254,203,167,211,
    254,16,254,36,13
100 DATA 32,226,201
110 DATA 58,72,92,31,31,31,
    230,7,225,229
120 DATA 95,14,0,22,15,126,
    230,16,131,211
130 DATA 254,65,16,254,35,
    21,32,243,13,32
140 DATA 238,201
150 FOR N=1 TO 3:
    RANDOMIZE USR 65206:
    RANDOMIZE USR 65247:
    NEXT N
```

You'll have got the idea about programs like this already. You're storing a routine – or in this case two routines – above RAMtop, and calling it with a RANDOMIZE USR call to the address it starts from. In this case we've got two machine code programs that will produce the sound of a laser burst and an explosion, in the case of the latter flashing the border to make the point.

Now if you count your way through the DATA statements you'll find the first routine, which ends at 65246, finishes at the end of line 100. The second ends at the end of 140, and you should now be able to see a similarity – both end with 201, and if you check that in the Z80 chip instruction set you'll find it means RET, or return. You'll find there are other numbers that repeat, and if you're going to get involved in machine code you'll become familiar with them, but at the moment it's just a matter of your being able to see a pattern.

In the case of the program here you should be able to detect a difference between what you can produce from Basic and what you get from machine code. In Basic you can use a FOR...NEXT loop to produce a series of notes, but they're separate notes – you can't produce anything like a smooth graduation. But machine code is much more flexible.

The Spectrum's BEEP is basically just a click. The speaker is connected to one of the output ports of the Z80, and whenever the speaker bit D4 is set a click is produced. The pitch of the note you hear is determined by the number of times per second D4 switches on and off. So instead of varying pitch and duration through Basic it's just a matter of varying the rate of clicking through machine code, and this produces a smoother variation in note.

The memory map

The diagram overleaf shows you how the Spectrum's memory is organised, and how the decimal numbers of the locations relate to the hexadecimal versions. In the interests of logic we'll deal with hex numbering here. The memory is best viewed as a long line of numbered boxes going from 0000h to FFFFh (7FFFh in the 16K Spectrum). Each of these boxes contains one 8-bit byte, known to mere mortals as an eight character binary number.

The memory is split up into Read Only Memory, the ROM, and Random Access Memory (RAM). You can change what's in RAM, but you can't change the ROM – you can, however use some of its built-in routines as we've shown you in the chapter on system variables.

The ROM runs from 0000h to 3FFFh – it is basically a set of programs written in Z80 machine language, and is arguably the one key feature that makes the Spectrum a Spectrum rather than, say, a Memotech. If you do get a thorough grounding in assembly language you'll find that various parts of the programs in the ROM can actually be used as subroutines in your own programs.

If you want to mess around seriously

with these, you'll need a disassembled listing of the Spectrum's ROM. A number of books containing these have been published, and, while they're not exactly easy to understand, a bit of application will pay dividends.

Just above the ROM in the memory you run into the fixed RAM. This is an area of RAM, within which fixed addresses are used by the ROM for things like the display and attributes files, which we covered in the chapter on colour. As far as we're concerned, the other important area here is the one holding the addresses used by the ROM to operate the Spectrum – these are the system variables.

Once you're through this section you get to the floating RAM, where the sections have no fixed length, although ROM keeps track of where they are by holding their addresses in the system variables. These sections include channel information and the Microdrive maps, and are followed by storage areas for Basic programs and their variables.

After this there are sections dealing with editing, temporary workspace and the calculator stack, and these are associated with the operation of Basic programs. The spare space above this varies in size depending on the size of the Basic program and the amount of variables it uses, but it can be used for storing data or for machine code programs.

Beyond this, and immediately below RAMtop, we have the machine stack and the GOSUB stack. Once you're out of this territory and beyond RAMtop you've left the area of memory which can be reset by NEW, so by lowering RAMtop with a CLEAR you're providing an area of memory that is protected against being overwritten by a totally Basic operation.

Incidentally, the user-defined graphics are normally just above RAMtop, which is why you can't reset them with NEW. The system variable UDG normally points at the first address of the user-defined graphics, but you can alter this to point somewhere else if necessary.

```
----------------------------------------        P_RAMT    FFFF    65536    ▲
    User-defined graphics                                                   |
----------------------------------------        RAMtop    FF57              |
    GOSUB stack                                                          Top end
----------------------------------------                                    |
    Machine stack                                                           |
----------------------------------------                                    ▼
                                                                            ▲
    Spare space                                                           Spare
----------------------------------------        STKEND                      ▼
```

Region	Label	Hex	Dec	Memory type
Calculator stack				
	STKBOT			
Temporary work space				
INPUT data				
	WORKSP			Floating RAM
Command or program line being edited				
	E_LINE			
Variables				
	VARS			
Basic program				
	PROG			
Channel information				
	CHANS			
Microdrive maps				
		5CB6	23734	
System variables				
		5C00	23552	Fixed RAM
Printer buffer				
		5B00	23296	
Attributes				
		5800	22528	
Display file				
		4000	16384	
Character set				
		3D00		ROM
Calculator				
		2C88		
Operating system and interpreter				
		0000	0000	

Checklist

In this chapter you should have learned:

☐ How the Spectrum's memory is laid out.

☐ How you can use POKE or an assembler to communicate with the memory, and to store programs in it.

☐ How to call machine code routines with RANDOMIZE USR.

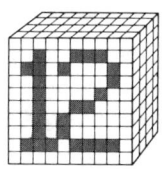

Sound

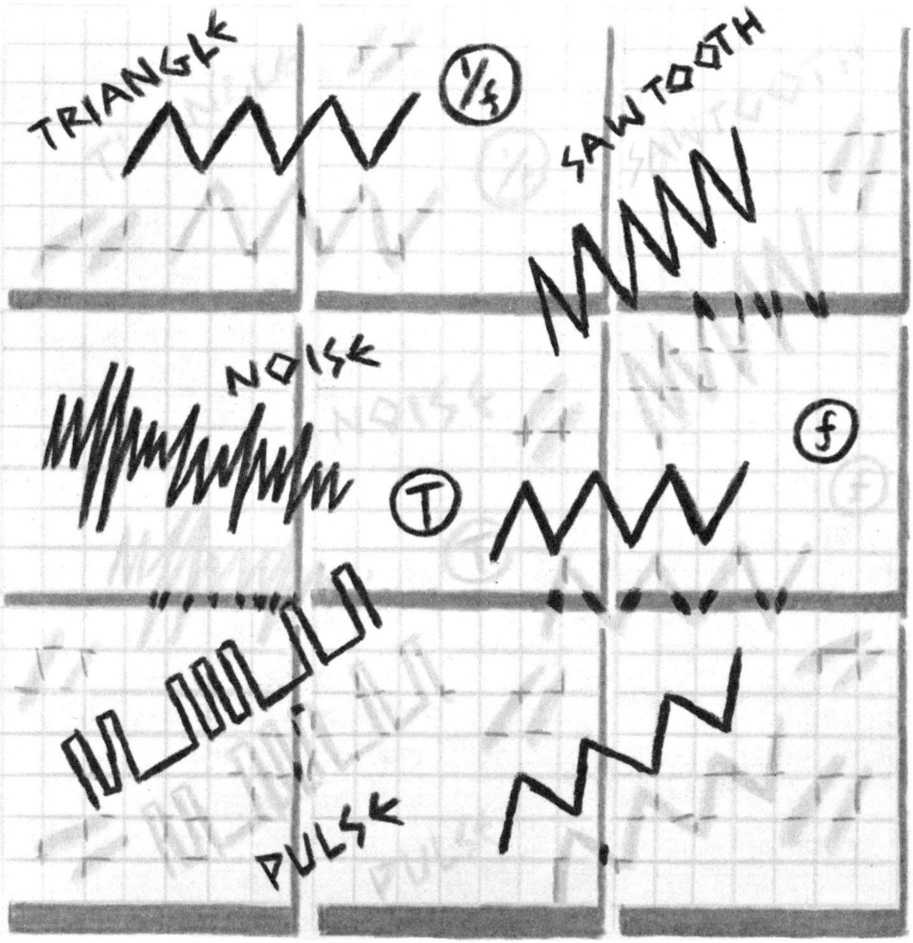

Computers are being used more and more to play music these days. The methods, and results, are many and varied. From semi-random notes to amazing gizmos, such as the Fairlight which can be used to record various sounds digitally, such as breaking glass, or barking dogs, and then play them back at different speeds to enable tunes to be played.

One of the advantages of music is that it can be represented in a number of different ways. All of these are numerically related, making them easy for a computer to handle. The difference between the notes in different octaves is related by frequency, i.e. the C above middle C is exactly twice the frequency. So, to move a note up an octave, simply multiply by two.

An octave is defined as being the interval between one frequency and its double, split into eight. In fact it is split into 13 semitones, the highest being twice the frequency of the first.

Unfortunately, this is where things begin to get a little more complex since the Western ear is used to a major scale of eight notes and, of course, there are thirteen. For example, listen to the following two programs:

```
10 FOR T=0 TO 12
20 BEEP .5,T
30 NEXT T
```

```
10 FOR T=0 TO 7
20 READ A
30 BEEP .5,A
40 NEXT T
50 DATA 0,2,4,5,7,9,11,12
```

The first plays all the semitones in the scale, the second plays only the major notes, that is, no sharps or flats.

To get around this, all keyboard instruments, such as pianos, harpsichords, and most synthesisers, have their keyboards split into two sections, the black notes, and the white notes. The former contain all the sharps and flats but, as we shall see later, this is relative to the key.

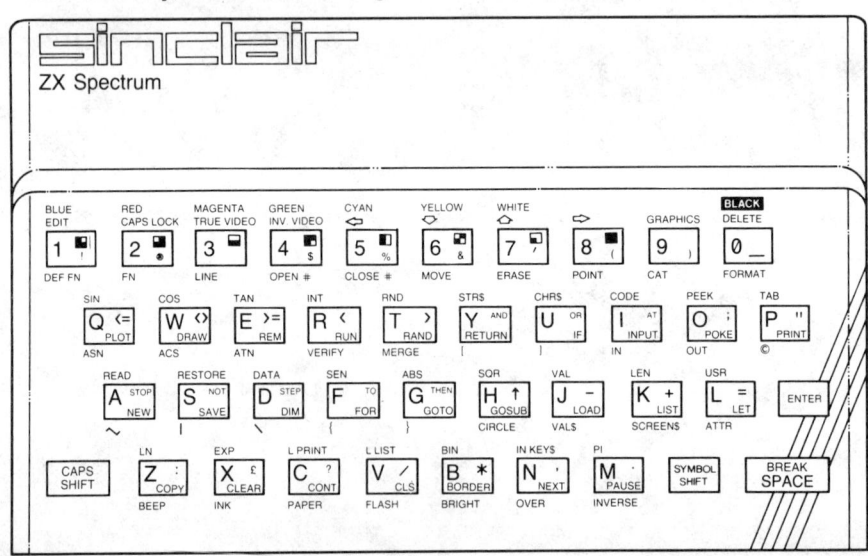

The intervals between E and F and B and C are taken to be semitones whereas the other intervals are full tones. The upshot of all this is the ease with which it is possible to play simple tunes in the key of C (no black notes). Most of the following programs will use only the major scale although it needn't be the key of C. Simply adding an offset to the value of the notes will change the key to be anything you wish. For instance, the following program, a development of the previous, demonstrates this.

```
10 FOR S=0 TO 12
20 FOR T=0 TO 7
30 READ A
40 BEEP .1,A+S
50 NEXT T
60 RESTORE
70 NEXT S
80 DATA 0,2,4,5,7,9,11,12
```

The Spectrum's typewriter keyboard can be set up to imitate a piano keyboard using the letters Q W E R T Y U I for the white notes, and 2 3 5 6 7 for the black. The layout will look like this:

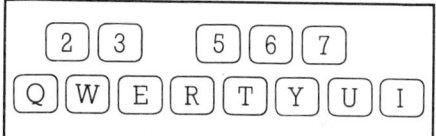

to give the notes

```
    C#  D#      F#  Ab  Bb
    C   D   E   F   G   A   B   C
```

A rather useful subroutine is one that decodes the keys and produces the appropriate note values. This is done by reading the keyboard with INKEY$ and then using the equality operator to pick/filter out the correct value. The note values are kept in an array for convenience, allowing them to be altered at will, without having to edit a great long Basic line. The routine is:

```
100 LET A$=INKEY$
110 IF A$="" THEN GOTO 100
115 LET N=((A$="Q")*S(1))+
    ((A$="2")*S(2))+((A$=
    "W")*S(3))+((A$="3")*
    S(4))+((A$="E")*
    S(5))+((A$="R")*S(6))
    +((A$="5")*S(7))+
    ((A$="T")*S(8))+
    ((A$="6")*S(9))
    +((A$="Y")*S(10))+
    ((A$="7")*S(11))+
    ((A$="U")*S(12))+
    ((A$="I")*S(13))
120 BEEP .1,N
130 GOTO 100
```

To set up the array, this next routine needs to be executed first.

```
1000 DIM S(13)
1010 FOR T=1 TO 13
1020 READ S(T)
1030 NEXT T
1040 RETURN
1050 DATA -3,-2,-1,0,1,2,3,
     4,5,6,7,8,9
```

The first line of the program should be:

```
10 LET A$="": GOSUB 1000
```

and you have a musical keyboard.
  There are a number of drawbacks to this program, not least its lack of flexibility.
  One problem is that the notes repeat far too quickly. A solution to this is to alter the following lines:

```
100 LET S$=A$:LET
    A$=INKEY$
```

```
106 IF S$=A$ THEN GOTO
    100
1005 LET A$=" "
```

which gets rid of the repeats altogether.

One of the other main problems with the Spectrum's sound command is that, once it starts, it can't be stopped, so make sure the note length in line 120 is not too long.

From here, a number of features can be added to make the program much more useful and versatile.

The first of these is a vibrato effect to make the sound a little more interesting. It would also be nice if this effect could be turned on and off. To get the vibrato, the beep frequency needs to be altered like this:

```
10 BEEP .01,0
20 BEEP .01,.7
30 GOTO 10
```

Using this idea, the following subroutine and lines can be added to get vibrato. It also offers a way around the problem of the note not being interrupted by another keypress. Since the actual BEEP is quite short, it is possible to detect another keypress halfway through and thus abort the current note for the next.

Another feature is the ability to tune the keyboard to any key or octave desired, and since there are now going to be quite a few functions, it's time to start defining some sort of menu system. Inserting the following lines starts us on our way.

```
10   LET A$="": GOSUB 1000
20   GOTO 3000
99   REM PLAY
106  IF S$=A$ THEN GOTO 100
107  IF A$="K" THEN RETURN
120  GOSUB 2000
160  RETURN
999  REM SET UP VARIABLES
     AND ARRAYS
1005 LET A$=""
1006 LET D=0:LET L=10:
     LET O=0
1999 REM NEW BEEP ROUTINE
2000 FOR T=0 TO L
2004 IF INKEY$="" THEN LET
     T=L:GOTO 2020
2005 BEEP.01,N+O
2010 BEEP.01,N+O+D
2020 NEXT T
2030 RETURN
2999 REM MAIN MENU
3000 CLS:PRINT" MAIN MENU"
3010 PRINT
3020 PRINT "Z...TUNE UP"
3030 PRINT "X...TUNE DOWN"
3040 PRINT "M...OCTAVE UP"
3050 PRINT "N...OCTAVE
     DOWN"
3060 PRINT "B...LENGTHEN
     NOTE"
3070 PRINT "V...SHORTEN
     NOTE"
3090 PRINT "S...INCREASE
     VIB DEPTH"
3100 PRINT "D...DECREASE
     VIB DEPTH"
3110 PRINT "L...PLAY"
3120 PRINT "K...MENU"
3200 LET A$=INKEY$
3210 IF A$="Z" THEN LET
     O=O+.5:GOSUB 3500:
     GOTO 3000
3220 IF A$="X" THEN LET
     O=O-.5:GOSUB 3500:
     GOTO 3000
3230 IF A$="M" THEN LET
     O=O+12:GOSUB 3500:
     GOTO 3000
3240 IF A$="N" THEN LET
     O=O-12:GOSUB 3500:
     GOTO 3000
3250 IF A$="B" THEN LET
     L=L+1:GOSUB 3600:
     GOTO 3000
3260 IF A$="V" THEN LET
     L=L-1:GOSUB 3600:
     GOTO 3000
3270 IF A$="S" THEN LET
     D=D+.1:GOSUB 3600:
     GOTO 3000
3280 IF A$="D" THEN LET
     D=D-.1:GOSUB 3600:
     GOTO 3000
3290 IF A$="L" THEN
     CLS:PRINT" PLAY":
     GOSUB 100:GOTO 3000
3300 GOTO 3200
3499 REM PLAY SCALE
3500 FOR N=0 TO 12
3510 GOSUB 2000
3520 NEXT N
3530 RETURN
3599 REM PLAY SINGLE NOTE
3600 LET N=0
3610 GOSUB 2000
3620 RETURN
```

This program now allows tunes to be played on the Spectrum keyboard, (use capital letters when you choose from the menu). The next thing to do is to allow them to be recorded and played back. There is also the opportunity here for allowing the notes to be shown on the screen in their proper place on the staff. The best way to do this is to use user-defined graphics like this:

```
4000 RESTORE 4000
4005 FOR T=0 TO 159
```

```
4010  READ A:POKE USR"A"+T,A
4020  NEXT T
4100  DATA 0,255,0,0,255,8,8,
      255,8,8,255,8,8,255,
      24,24
4110  DATA 0,255,0,8,255,8,8,
      255,8,8,255,8,24,255,
      24,0
4120  DATA 0,255,8,8,255,8,8,
      255,8,8,255,24,24,255,
      0,0
4130  DATA 0,255,8,8,255,8,8,
      255,8,24,255,24,0,255,
      0,0
4140  DATA 8,255,8,8,255,8,8,
      255,24,24,255,0,0,255,
      0,0
4145  DATA 0,255,0,0,255,0,
      24,255,24,16,255,16,
      16,255,16,16
4150  DATA 0,255,0,0,255,24,
      24,255,16,16,255,16,
      16,255,16,16
4160  DATA 0,255,0,24,255,24,
      16,255,16,16,255,16,
      16,255,16,0
4170  DATA 0,255,24,24,255,
      16,16,255,16,16,255,16,
      16,255,0,0
4180  DATA 24,255,24,16,255,
      16,16,255,16,16,255,16,
      0,255,0,0
4190  RETURN
```

Once these are in, they can be used with the following subroutine.
Note that the characters in lines 4205 and 4210 are graphics characters (UDGs).

```
4200  LET G=G+1:IF G>30
      THEN LET M=M+3:
      LET G=0
4201  IF M>21 THEN LET
      M=2:LET G=0
4205  PRINT AT M,G;("A" AND
      N=-3);("C" AND N=-1);
```

```
      ("E" AND N=1);("G" AND
      N=2);("I" AND N=4);
      ("K" AND N=6);("M" AND
      N=8);("O" AND N=10);
4210  PRINT AT M+1,G;("B"
      AND N=-3);("D" AND
      N=-1);("F" AND N=1);
      ("H" AND N=2);("J" AND
      N=4);("L" AND N=6);
      ("N" AND N=8);("P"
      AND N=10);
4220  RETURN
```

To use this we must also add the following lines.

```
1007  LET M=2:LET G=0
 125  GOSUB 4200
  11  GOSUB 4000
```

and change line 3290

```
3290  IF A$="L" THEN LET
      M=2:LET G=0:CLS:GOSUB
      100:GOTO 3000
```

Now, whenever a note is played, the appropriate music comes up on the screen. To record the notes, they must be stored in an array so let's set up array Q() and provide a facility load and save tunes from tape or Microdrive. Add to the main menu:

```
3130  PRINT "G...TUNE EDIT
      MENU"
3295  IF A$="G" THEN GOSUB
      6000:REM TUNE EDIT MENU
6000  CLS
6010  PRINT"TUNE EDIT MENU"
6020  PRINT
6030  PRINT"A...NEW TUNE"
6040  PRINT"B...PLAY BACK
      TUNE"
6050  PRINT"C...EDIT TUNE"
6060  PRINT"D...SAVE TUNE"
6070  PRINT"E...LOAD TUNE"
6080  PRINT"0...MAIN MENU"
6200  LET A$=INKEY$
6210  IF A$="A" THEN GOSUB
      6300:GOTO 6000
6220  IF A$="B" THEN GOSUB
      6400:GOTO 6000
6230  IF A$="C" THEN GOSUB
      6700:GOTO 6000
6240  IF A$="D" THEN GOSUB
      6500:GOTO 6000
6250  IF A$="E" THEN GOSUB
      6600:GOTO 6000
6255  IF A$="0" THEN RETURN
6260  GOTO 6200
6299  REM NEW TUNE
6300  LET R=1:REM SET RECORD
      FLAG
6310  LET C=1:LET M=2:LET
      G=0:CLS:GOSUB 100
6320  LET NTS=C:LET R=0
6330  RETURN
```

Add in a line 126

```
126   IF R=1 THEN LET
      Q(C)=N:LET C=C+1
```

and lines

```
1001  DIM Q(64)
1008  LET R=0:LET NTS=1
6399  REM PLAY BACK TUNE
6400  CLS:PRINT"HOLD B DOWN
      TO HEAR TUNE"
6410  LET M=2:LET G=0
6420  FOR C=1 TO NTS
6430  LET N=Q(C):GOSUB 2000:
      GOSUB 4200
6440  NEXT C
6445  GOSUB 1500
6450  RETURN
```

Insert lines:

```
1500  PRINT AT 21,0;"PRESS
      SPACE TO CONTINUE"
1510  IF INKEY$<>" " THEN
      GOTO 1510
1520  RETURN
6499  REM SAVE THAT TUNE
6500  INPUT"ENTER FILE NAME ";
      F$
6510  SAVE *"M";1;F$ DATA Q()
6520  RETURN
6599  REM LOAD THAT TUNE
6600  INPUT"ENTER FILE NAME ";
      F$
6610  LOAD *"M";1;F$ DATA Q()
6620  RETURN
```

To allow editing, some of the program must be changed around a little. The only routine that needs altering is to make line 115 a subroutine in its own right. Simply LIST 115 and then edit it. Change the line number to 150 and change 115 to GOSUB 150. Then make a new line 160 RETURN.

This allows the keyboard reading routine to be used separately.

```
6699  REM EDIT THAT TUNE
6700  CLS:PRINT" STEP
      THROUGH THE TUNE
      BY":PRINT" PRESSING
      SPACE. USE 'X' TO EXIT."
6710  PRINT"TO CHANGE A
      NOTE, PRESS THE NEW
      NOTE KEY "
6715  LET M=8:LET G=0
6720  FOR C=1 TO 64
6730  LET N=Q(C):GOSUB
      4200:BEEP .1,N
6740  LET A$=INKEY$:IF A$=""
      THEN GOTO 6740
6745  IF A$="X" THEN LET
      C=64
6750  IF A$<>" " THEN GOSUB
      150:BEEP .1,N:LET
      Q(C)=N:LET G=G-1:
      GOSUB 4200
6755  IF C>NTS THEN LET
      NTS=NTS+1
6770  NEXT C
6780  RETURN
```

Obviously, improvements can be made to this program but it does lay the basis for a composing program. The way in which it was constructed shows some of the methods of program modification and construction. Particularly the need for documenting the program with REMs.

The main use of the Spectrum's sound generator is to create background noises for games, i.e. zaps, bangs, kapows etc. Most of these are easy to construct and are documented in many other books and manuals. For completeness, we will include a few such effects here, to give you an idea of what can be achieved. For instance, a spaceship taking off:

```
10  FOR T=0 TO 69
20  FOR S=0 TO 5
30  BEEP .005,T
40  NEXT S
50  NEXT T
```

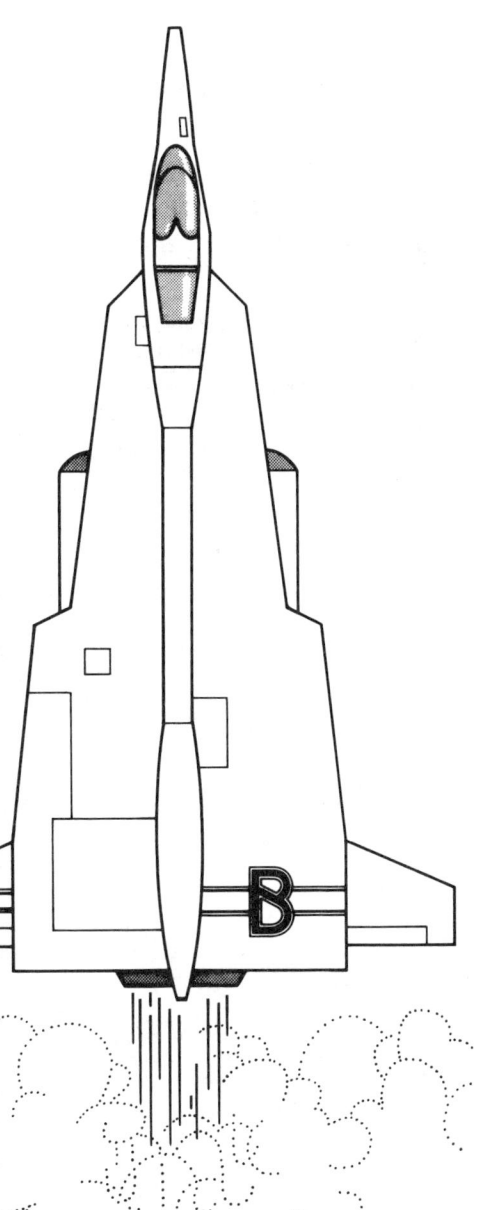

To land it simply change the first line to:

```
10  FOR T=69 TO 0 STEP -1
```

To get a fire engine on the scene, use

```
10  BEEP .5,10
20  BEEP .5,5
30  GOTO 10
```

For more effective noises, it is better to access the Spectrum's speaker directly. Using the OUT(254) instruction this can be done fairly easily. Unfortunately, the border colour is also controlled from here so we must OUT the correct colour as well as the sound. For example:

```
10  OUT 254,16
20  OUT 254,0
30  GOTO 10
```

gives a nice machine type sound but the border changes colour. The first three bits of the byte that is output control the red, blue and green colours. To maintain the current border colour you must make sure that the mix is correct. This can be achieved with a little experimentation. Try this:

```
10  FOR T=0 TO 7
20  OUT 254,T
25  PRINT T
30  PAUSE 0
40  NEXT T
```

This shows the colours that can be obtained. Simply adding or subtracting 16 from the selected colour number turns the speaker on and off. So selecting a white border for the machine sound program is done like this:

```
10  OUT 254,23
20  OUT 254,7
30  GOTO 10
```

where 23 is 16+7. If you alter line 10 to OUT 254,16+7 you will notice a change in the frequency of the sound due to the Spectrum having to evaluate 16+7 every time it goes through the loop.

To get a Geiger counter moving away from a radiation source we can use:

```
10 FOR T=0 TO 100
20 OUT 254,23
30 OUT 254,7
40 FOR S=0 TO T:NEXT S
50 NEXT T
```

and to get random pulses:

```
10 OUT 254,23:OUT 254,7
20 FOR T=0 TO INT
   (RND*10)-1:NEXT T
30 GOTO 10
```

The amount by which RND is multiplied gives the average frequency of these pulses.

There are many more tricks that can be achieved by accessing the OUT 254 directly but to get any good effects it is usually necessary to resort to machine code. Such things as white noise, and cricket or helicopter sounds are then possible but the means are a little beyond this book.

Projects

☐ Improve on the music composer program to give a full screen editor to change the notes and allow them to be printed out (try the COPY command). The composer program could also be modified to produce sharps and flats with the graphics, although you will probably need to redefine the main character set to get enough graphics characters.

☐ Experiment with the BEEP command to get various sound effects, then modify your programs to do the same thing with OUT 254.

☐ Look up pulse width modulation and see how this can be used to enable the Spectrum to produce speech.

13

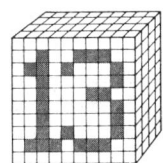

Interface 1 and interfacing

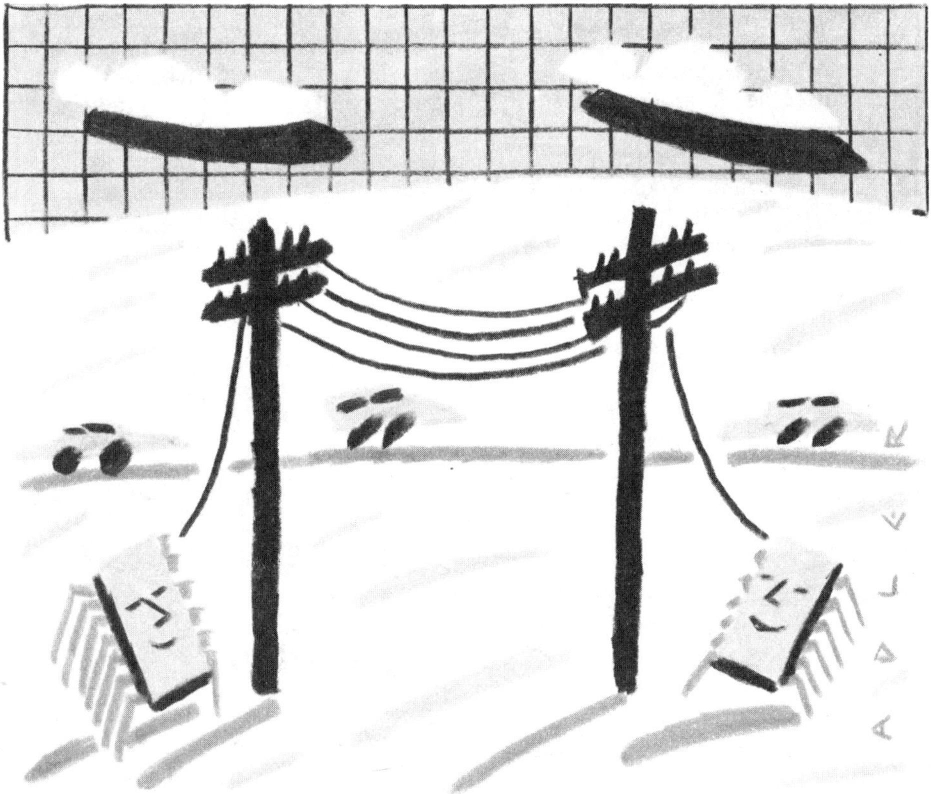

The Spectrum that you buy in the shops is excellent value, but after you've done a bit of programming on it you'll run into a couple of major disadvantages, including the difficulty involved in producing a printout and the slow loading and saving times associated with tape storage. The popularity of the Spectrum has meant that a number of solutions to these problems have been developed, not least of them being Sinclair's own Interface 1.

The essential add-on

To understand what Interface 1 is you have to look a little at the basic design of the Spectrum. The machine as it stands is a self-contained unit that communicates with the outside world only through its TV output and its tape sockets. At the back of the machine there is also something called an 'edge connector' which is basically an extension of the computer's main circuit board. If you look at this you'll see a number of lines which are potentially communications channels.

On more expensive computers these lines are formed into a number of sockets that allow you to plug into printers, monitors and so on, but you can see that it's actually a lot cheaper just to design the circuit board so that these lines project out of a hole in the back of the machine, and worry about the plugs later.

What Interface 1 does is to take these lines and use them for three specific purposes – a printer interface, control of the Sinclair Microdrives, and a networking facility. It's worth looking at these three areas in a little more detail.

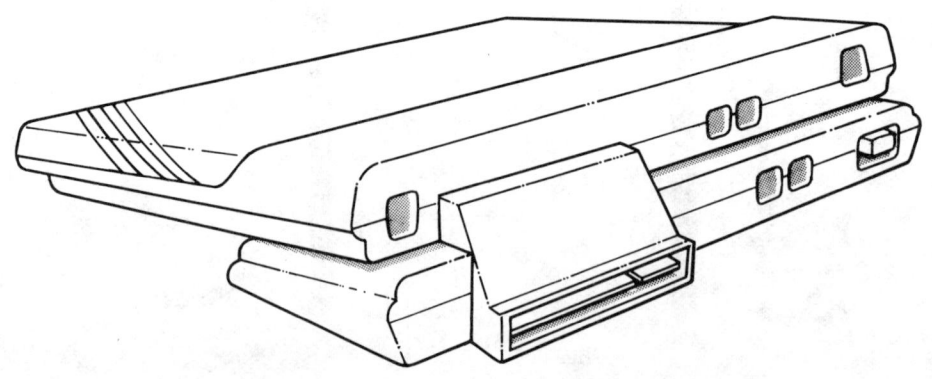

The printer interface

There are essentially two standard printer interfaces for use with computers, Centronics, or parallel, and RS232, or serial. Interface 1 uses the latter. Without getting too technical the easiest way to explain the difference between these is that a parallel interface sends data along a number of lines simultaneously while a serial interface sends data along one line. You can vary the speed and form of data transfer with a serial interface, but you cannot with a parallel interface.

Now a consequence of this is that you can use a variety of methods to carry serial data – you can send it along telephone lines, for example, simply by converting the signal to sound and back again. The RS232 therefore gives you the opportunity to communicate with other micros, or with devices like robots and burglar alarms. So RS232 is about communications and control, and all you need do to open this world up is to write the software!

If you simply want a printer interface in order to produce written output, for word processing or for listing your programs, the Centronics interface is probably more convenient. It lacks the flexibility of RS232, but because you do not have to set data transfer rates it is often less trouble to use. Although Interface 1 doesn't have this facility you can get Centronics interfaces for the Spectrum, and you'll find a number of these listed at the end of this chapter.

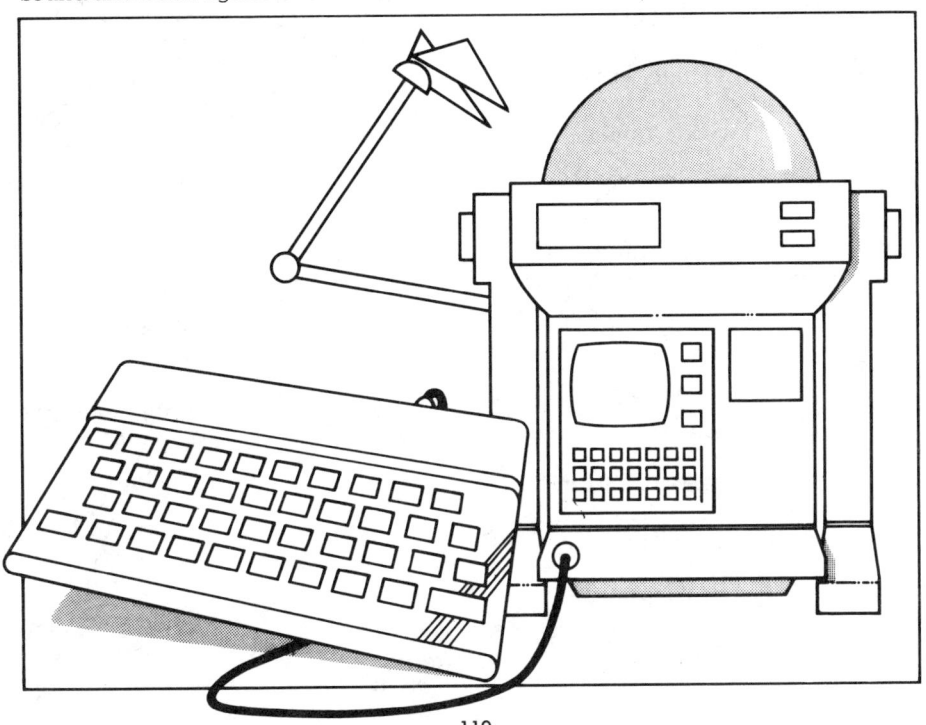

Interface 1 and interfacing

The network

Interface 1 includes a facility for something called a 'local area network' – this is essentially a group of computers operating within cable-length of one another, and linked by those cables. Sinclair's system will support anything from two to sixty-four Spectrums linked in this way, and, although there are things you and a few friends could use the network for, the most obvious application is in schools.

The basic use of the network is straightforward, and employs versions of other Spectrum/Interface 1 commands for control purposes. In order to send information, for example you use a variation on the SAVE command, while to receive you use LOAD – the only difference is that you're SAVEing to and LOADing from a Spectrum, rather than tape.

If you do have a number of friends who own Interface 1 then it might be worthwhile to develop some form of interactive game that would allow you to use the networking facility – there are already a few of these being sold commercially, but there are plenty of ideas that could still be developed.

The Microdrives

The idea of the Sinclair Microdrive is that it should provide a cheap and effective alternative to disk storage, and broadly speaking it does this. The basic unit is a black box about the size of your fist that will take a small cartridge containing a continuous tape loop. With disk storage you can usually

load programs by using 'random access' – i.e. the disk drive unit can go to any part of the disk to pick up the information to be loaded, rather like a record player can.

With tape units you have to wind through the whole of the tape to get to a particular program. The Microdrive is a tape unit, but has the advantage that it runs so fast that it only takes eight seconds or so to go through the entire tape – its access times are therefore comparable to those of some disk drive units.

TRY THIS

Because of the improved access times it's feasible to do things with Microdrives that you cannot do with tape. Let's say you want a way to display your artistic talents to your friends, and although you have an excellent drawing program, you've just got so many pictures you can't fit them all in memory at once:

```
 10  CLS
 20  PRINT
 30  PRINT "FILM SHOW"
 40  PRINT
 50  INPUT "ENTER NUMBER OF
         PICTURES ON
         CARTRIDGE";A$
 60  IF VAL A$<1 OR VAL
         A$>20 THEN BEEP 1,1:
         GO TO 50
 70  LET A=VAL A$: CLS
 80  PRINT
 90  PRINT "SELECT MODE"
100  PRINT "1...FOR
         CONTINUOUS SHOW"
105  PRINT "2...FOR PAUSE
         BETWEEN PICTURES"
```

Interface 1 and interfacing

```
110 PRINT "3...TO SELECT A
    PICTURE"
120 IF INKEY$="1" THEN FOR
    N=1 TO A: LOAD *"M";1;
    STR$(N) SCREEN$:
    NEXT N
130 IF INKEY$="2" THEN FOR
    N=1 TO A: LOAD
    *"M";1;STR$(N)SCREEN$:
    PAUSE 0: NEXT N
140 IF INKEY$="3" THEN
    PRINT: INPUT "PICTURE
    NUMBER? ";N: LOAD
    *"M";1;STR$(N) SCREEN$
150 GO TO 90
```

What you've got here is the basis of an interesting little slide show program. You'll see it's a lot faster than tape, but it's still a little slow. But as you know the Spectrum has the space in memory to hold a number of screens at one time, so you could use the program here as the basis for a sort of animated sequence. As it stands the program can be used to recall any SCREEN$ saved as a number. If you want to do anything cleverer though you should be able to work it out.

The commands

```
FORMAT "M";N;"NAME"
CAT N
ERASE "M";N;"FILENAME"
SAVE *"M";N;"FILENAME"
LOAD *"M";N;"FILENAME"
VERIFY *"M";N;"FILENAME"
MERGE *"M";N;"FILENAME"
```

As you can see from the table the basic Microdrive handling commands, with the addition of FORMAT, CAT and ERASE, are similar to the Spectrum's tape handling commands, although the syntax is more complicated. You must specify a filename when loading, saving etc., and you must also specify the Microdrive number (N in the table).

The Interface 1 unit has its own ROM, and this is switched into the Spectrum's ROM as a sort of error intercept. Normally you'll get an error message if you try to use a Microdrive command, but with Interface 1 connected the Spectrum checks with the Interface 1 ROM first, and if the

command is in fact OK it executes it. Note that there could be a useful bonus here – if you can head off the ROM routines dealing with this you could actually add your own commands to the Spectrum.

Interface 2

The second Spectrum peripheral device of interest to us is Interface 2. This is simpler than Interface 1 in that it only provides two extra facilities, for ROM cartridges and joysticks. The ROM cartridges are useful in that they are the fastest possible way to load a game, by virtue of the fact that they're actually switching in an area of memory, but it's not possible for you to SAVE your own programs onto them.

The cartridges do however open a number of opportunities for things like switching in whole new operating systems for the Spectrum, and no doubt one day someone will start selling something like this.

The joysticks however are something you can incorporate in your programs. The following table shows how the two joysticks relate to the Spectrum's keyboard:

Key	Joystick movement	Joystick
1	Left	2
2	Right	2
3	Down	2
4	Up	2
5	Fire	2
6	Left	1
7	Right	1
8	Down	1
9	Up	1
0	Fire	1

So if you plug two joysticks into Interface 2 you'll get the same effect as using these keys, provided, of course, your program allows for it.

Normally you'd use INKEY$ to do this, but this has the disadvantage of being unable to read two key presses at the same time, so it's not possible to move and fire at the same time. There is, however, another command that can be used.

The function IN and the statement OUT are used to control the Input/Output (I/O) ports of the Spectrum. By typing:

IN address

you can get the byte from the port whose address you use returned. You write to that port by using:

OUT address, value

The one that concerns us at the moment is IN. The addresses governing the two joystick ports are 61438 for joystick 1 and 63486 for 2. So saying IN 61438 will return us an eight bit number giving us information on the status of joystick 1. There are five movements to be governed by the port, so it's only the first five of the eight bits we're interested in:

Movement	Joystick 1 IN 61438	Joystick 2 IN 63486
Fire	Bit 0	Bit 4
Up	Bit 1	Bit 3
Down	Bit 2	Bit 2
Right	Bit 3	Bit 1
Left	Bit 4	Bit 0

The situation here is analogous to that of the KSTATE system variables. By moving joystick 1 you change the number held in 61438, and as you see from the table above each of the first five bits of that number governs one particular action. So in order to use IN to move something on the screen we have to examine these bits individually. First we need a variable for each movement:

```
10 LET F=0: LET U=0: LET
   D=0: LET R=0: LET L=0
```

Here we've got five variables, one for each movement, and we've set them to zero, i.e. stationary. The next step is to read the value at 61438, and remove the bits 5, 6 and 7, as we don't want them:

```
20 LET N=255-IN 61438
30 IF N>127 THEN LET
   N=N-128
40 IF N>63 THEN LET
   N=N-64
50 IF N>31 THEN LET
   N=N-32
```

We now have all the bits we want. So now we read them individually, and modify the state of our five variables depending on what's being done with the stick:

```
60 IF N>15 THEN LET
   N=N-16: LET L=1
70 IF N>7 THEN LET N=N-8:
   LET R=1
80 IF N>3 THEN LET N=N-4:
   LET D=1
90 IF N>1 THEN LET N=N-2:
   LET U=1
100 IF N=1 THEN LET F=1
```

All you need do now is to write a topsy-turvy routine for joystick 2, and plug in the movement based on the values of the variables.

Other peripherals

This book isn't really the place for a buyer's guide to Spectrum peripherals, but there are a number of things you might be interested in learning more about. Should you wish to get yourself a Centronics interface, either instead of or in addition to Interface 1 then switchable Centronics/RS232 interfaces are manufactured by Euroelectronics and Morex. Both these are compatible with Interface 1, and this is important, as peripherals made by some companies will not work with Interface 1 connected.

Two other devices you may be interested in are a monitor and a proper keyboard for the Spectrum. In most cases a new keyboard will mean invalidating your Spectrum's guarantee, as you'll have to open the case, but this is unnecessary in a few cases. Probably the best of the ones that force you to open your Spectrum is made by Transform, and of those that don't the Stonechip is one you might like to look at.

You can really only connect a monitor if you know a little about soldering, or you know someone who does. Look at the plan of the edge connector at the end of chapter 23 of the Spectrum manual and you'll see where two lines are, Video and 0V. Connect the Video line to the central core of your TV cable and 0V to the outside, and you have a composite video output. In the case of the issue 3 Spectrum (if you've bought your Spectrum any time since Christmas 1983 it will be an issue 3) this is all you need to do, but there is another

connection to make on earlier models.
In any event, don't do this unless you
know exactly what you're doing.

There are plenty more add-ons you
can buy for the Spectrum, and if you do
want to expand your system the best
thing you can do is keep an eye on
what's being written and advertised in
the specialist Sinclair magazines. You
should also be able to find the
addresses of the companies
mentioned above. One last word of
warning – always make sure the
company is still in business, and that it
stocks the product you want, before
sending money through the post, and
you'll save yourself a lot of
disappointment.

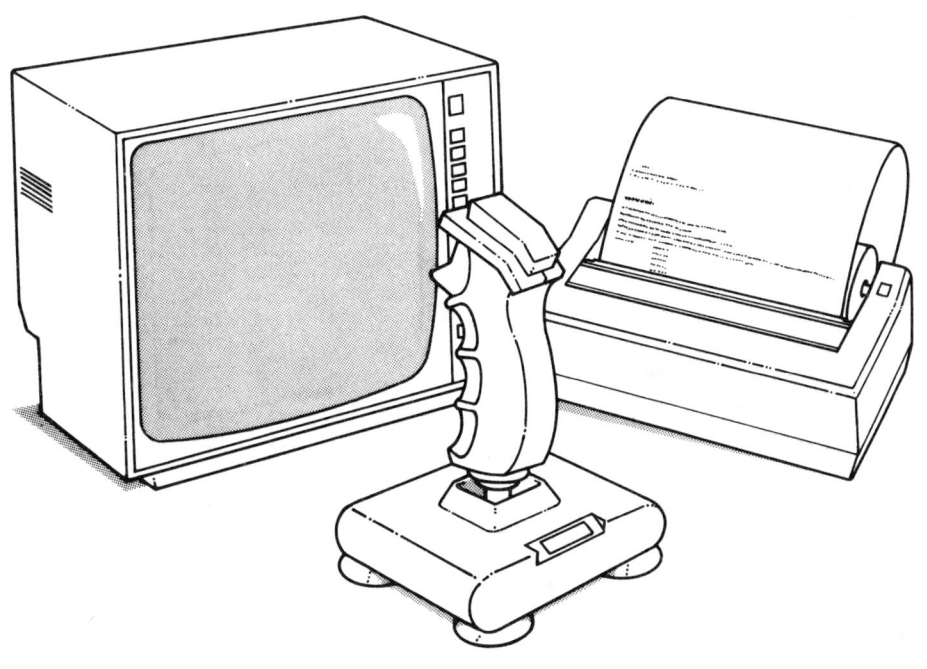

Checklist

In this chapter you should have learned:

- [ ] The difference between an RS232 and a Centronics interface.
- [ ] What a local area network is.
- [ ] The difference between Random Access and Serial Access.
- [ ] How to tailor your programs so they work with Interface 2.

Appendix

ASCII codes of the Spectrums character set

Code	Character	Hex	Z80 Assembler	– after CB	– after ED
0	⎤	00	NOP	RLC B	
1	⎟	01	LD BC,nn	RLC C	
2	⎟ not used	02	LD (BC),A	RLC D	
3	⎟	03	INC BC	RLC E	
4	⎟	04	INC B	RLC H	
5	⎦	05	DEC B	RLC L	
6	**PRINT** comma	06	LD B,n	RLC (HL)	
7	**EDIT**	07	RLCA	RLC A	
8	cursor left	08	EX AF,AF'	RRC B	
9	cursor right	09	ADD HL,BC	RRC C	
10	cursor down	0A	LD A,(BC)	RRC D	
11	cursor up	0B	DEC BC	RRC E	
12	**DELETE**	0C	INC C	RRC H	
13	**ENTER**	0D	DEC C	RRC L	
14	number	0E	LD C,n	RRC (HL)	
15	not used	0F	RRCA	RRC A	
16	**INK** control	10	DJNZ n	RL B	
17	**PAPER** control	11	LD DE,nn	RL C	
18	**FLASH** control	12	LD (DE),A	RL D	
19	**BRIGHT** control	13	INC DE	RL E	
20	**INVERSE** control	14	INC D	RL H	
21	**OVER** control	15	DEC D	RL L	
22	**AT** control	16	LD D,n	RL (HL)	
23	**TAB** control	17	RLA	RL A	
24	⎤	18	JR n	RR B	
25	⎟	19	ADD HL,DE	RR C	
26	⎟	1A	LD A,(DE)	RR D	
27	⎟ not used	1B	DEC DE	RR E	
28	⎟	1C	INC E	RR H	
29	⎟	1D	DEC E	RR L	
30	⎟	1E	LD E,n	RR (HL)	
31	⎦	1F	RRA	RR A	
32	space	20	JR NZ,n	SLA B	
33	!	21	LD HL,nn	SLA C	
34	"	22	LD (nn),HL	SLA D	
35	#	23	INC HL	SLA E	
36	$	24	INC H	SLA H	
37	%	25	DEC H	SLA L	
38	&	26	LD H,n	SLA (HL)	
39	'	27	DAA	SLA A	
40	(	28	JR Z,n	SRA B	
41	)	29	ADD HL,HL	SRA C	

Code	Character	Hex	Z80 Assembler	– after CB	– after ED
42	*	2A	LD HL,(nn)	SRA D	
43	+	2B	DEC HL	SRA E	
44	,	2C	INC L	SRA H	
45	–	2D	DEC L	SRA L	
46	.	2E	LD L,n	SRA (HL)	
47	/	2F	CPL	SRA A	
48	0	30	JR NC,n		
49	1	31	LD SP,nn		
50	2	32	LD (nn),A		
51	3	33	INC SP		
52	4	34	INC (HL)		
53	5	35	DEC (HL)		
54	6	36	LD (HL),n		
55	7	37	SCF		
56	8	38	JR C,n	SRL B	
57	9	39	ADD HL,SP	SRL C	
58	:	3A	LD A,(nn)	SRL D	
59	;	3B	DEC SP	SRL E	
60	<	3C	INC A	SRL H	
61	=	3D	DEC A	SRL L	
62	>	3E	LD A,n	SRL (HL)	
63	?	3F	CCF	SRL A	
64	@	40	LD B,D	BIT 0,B	IN B,(C)
65	A	41	LD B,C	BIT 0,C	OUT (C),B
66	B	42	LD B,D	BIT 0,D	SBC HL,BC
67	C	43	LD B,E	BIT 0,E	LD (nn),BC
68	D	44	LD B,H	BIT 0,H	NEG
69	E	45	LD B,L	BIT 0,L	RETN
70	F	46	LD B,(HL)	BIT 0,(HL)	IM 0
71	G	47	LD B,A	BIT 0,A	LD I,A
72	H	48	LD C,B	BIT 1,B	IN C,(C)
73	I	49	LD C,C	BIT 1,C	OUT (C),C
74	J	4A	LD C,D	BIT 1,D	ADC HL,BC
75	K	4B	LD C,E	BIT 1,E	LD BC,(nn)
76	L	4C	LD C,H	BIT 1,H	
77	M	4D	LD C,L	BIT 1,L	RETI
78	N	4E	LD C,(HL)	BIT 1,(HL)	
79	O	4F	LD C,A	BIT 1,A	LD R,A
80	P	50	LD D,B	BIT 2,B	IN D,(C)
81	Q	51	LD D,C	BIT 2,C	OUT (C),D
82	R	52	LD D,D	BIT 2,D	SBC HL,DE
83	S	53	LD D,E	BIT 2,E	LD (nn),DE

Code	Character	Hex	Z80 Assembler	– after CB	– after ED
84	T	54	LD D,H	BIT 2,H	
85	U	55	LD D,L	BIT 2,L	
86	V	56	LD D,(HL)	BIT 2,(HL)	IM 1
87	W	57	LD D,A	BIT 2,A	LD A,I
88	X	58	LD E,B	BIT 3,B	IN E,(C)
89	Y	59	LD E,C	BIT 3,C	OUT (C),E
90	Z	5A	LD E,D	BIT 3,D	ADC HL,DE
91	[	5B	LD E,E	BIT 3,E	LD DE,(nn)
92	/	5C	LD E,H	BIT 3,H	
93	]	5D	LD E,L	BIT 3,L	
94	↑	5E	LD E,(HL)	BIT 3,(HL)	IM 2
95	—	5F	LD E, A	BIT 3,A	LD A,R
96	£	60	LD H,B	BIT 4,B	IN H,(C)
97	a	61	LD H,C	BIT 4,C	OUT (C),H
98	b	62	LD H,D	BIT 4,D	SBC HL,HL
99	c	63	LD H,E	BIT 4,E	LD (nn),HL
100	d	64	LD H,H	BIT 4,H	
101	e	65	LD H,L	BIT 4,L	
102	f	66	LD H,(HL)	BIT 4,(HL)	
103	g	67	LD H,A	BIT 4,A	RRD
104	h	68	LD L,B	BIT 5,B	IN L,(C)
105	i	69	LD L,C	BIT 5,C	OUT (C),L
106	j	6A	LD L,D	BIT 5,D	ADC HL,HL
107	k	6B	LD L,E	BIT 5,E	LD HL,(nn)
108	l	6C	LD L,H	BIT 5,H	
109	m	6D	LD L,L	BIT 5,L	
110	n	6E	LD L,(HL)	BIT 5,(HL)	
111	o	6F	LD L,A	BIT 5,A	RLD
112	p	70	LD (HL),B	BIT 6,B	IN F,(C)
113	q	71	LD (HL),C	BIT 6,C	
114	r	72	LD (HL),D	BIT 6,D	SBC HL,SP
115	s	73	LD (HL),E	BIT 6,E	LD (nn),SP
116	t	74	LD (HL),H	BIT 6,H	
117	u	75	LD (HL),L	BIT 6,L	
118	v	76	HALT	BIT 6,(HL)	
119	w	77	LD (HL),A	BIT 6,A	
120	x	78	LD A,B	BIT 7,B	IN A,(C)
121	y	79	LD A,C	BIT 7,C	OUT (C),A
122	z	7A	LD A,D	BIT 7,D	ADC HL,SP
123	{	7B	LD A,E	BIT 7,E	LD SP,(nn)
124	|	7C	LD A,H	BIT 7,H	
125	}	7D	LD A,L	BIT 7,L	
126	~	7E	LD A,(HL)	BIT 7,(HL)	
127	©	7F	LD A,A	BIT 7,A	

Code	Character	Hex	Z80 Assembler	– after CB	– after ED
128	□	80	ADD A,B	RES 0,B	
129	▘	81	ADD A,C	RES 0,C	
130	▝	82	ADD A,D	RES 0,D	
131	▀	83	ADD A,E	RES 0,E	
132	▖	84	ADD A,H	RES 0,H	
133	▌	85	ADD A,L	RES 0,L	
134	▞	86	ADD A,(HL)	RES 0,(HL)	
135	▛	87	ADD A,A	RES 0,A	
136	▗	88	ADC A,B	RES 1,B	
137	▚	89	ADC A,C	RES 1,C	
138	▐	8A	ADC A,D	RES 1,D	
139	▜	8B	ADC A,E	RES 1,E	
140	▄	8C	ADC A,H	RES 1,H	
141	▙	8D	ADC A,L	RES 1,L	
142	▟	8E	ADC A,(HL)	RES 1,(HL)	
143	■	8F	ADC A,A	RES 1,A	
144	(a)	90	SUB B	RES 2,B	
145	(b)	91	SUB C	RES 2,C	
146	(c)	92	SUB D	RES 2,D	
147	(d)	93	SUB E	RES 2,E	
148	(e)	94	SUB H	RES 2,H	
149	(f)	95	SUB L	RES 2,L	
150	(g)	96	SUB (HL)	RES 2,(HL)	
151	(h)	97	SUB A	RES 2,A	
152	(i)	98	SBC A,B	RES 3,B	
153	(j)	99	SBC A,C	RES 3,C	
154	(k)	9A	SBC A,D	RES 3,D	
155	(l)	9B	SBC A,E	RES 3,E	
156	(m)	9C	SBC A,H	RES 3,H	
157	(n)	9D	SBC A,L	RES 3,L	
158	(o)	9E	SBC A,(HL)	RES 3,(HL)	
159	(p)	9F	SBC A,A	RES 3,A	
160	(q)	A0	AND B	RES 4,B	LDI
161	(r)	A1	AND C	RES 4,C	CPI
162	(s)	A2	AND D	RES 4,D	INI
163	(t)	A3	AND E	RES 4,E	OUTI
164	(u)	A4	AND H	RES 4,H	
165	**RND**	A5	AND L	RES 4,L	
166	**INKEY$**	A6	AND (HL)	RES 4,(HL)	
167	**PI**	A7	AND A	RES 4,A	
168	**FN**	A8	XOR B	RES 5,B	LDD
169	**POINT**	A9	XOR C	RES 5,C	CPD
170	**SCREEN$**	AA	XOR D	RES 5,D	IND
171	**ATTR**	AB	XOR E	RES 5,E	OUTD

Codes 144–164 are user graphics.

Code	Character	Hex	Z80 Assembler	– after CB	– after ED
172	**AT**	AC	XOR H	RES 5,H	
173	**TAB**	AD	XOR L	RES 5,L	
174	**VAL$**	AE	XOR (HL)	RES 5,(HL)	
175	**CODE**	AF	XOR A	RES 5,A	
176	**VAL**	B0	OR B	RES 6,B	LDIR
177	**LEN**	B1	OR C	RES 6,C	CPIR
178	**SIN**	B2	OR D	RES 6,D	INIR
179	**COS**	B3	OR E	RES 6,E	OTIR
180	**TAN**	B4	OR H	RES 6,H	
181	**ASN**	B5	OR L	RES 6,L	
182	**ACS**	B6	OR (HL)	RES 6,(HL)	
183	**ATN**	B7	OR A	RES 6,A	
184	**LN**	B8	CP B	RES 7,B	LDDR
185	**EXP**	B9	CP C	RES 7,C	CPDR
186	**INT**	BA	CP D	RES 7,D	INDR
187	**SQR**	BB	CP E	RES 7,E	OTDR
188	**SGN**	BC	CP H	RES 7,H	
189	**ABS**	BD	CP L	RES 7,L	
190	**PEEK**	BE	CP (HL)	RES 7,(HL)	
191	**IN**	BF	CP A	RES 7,A	
192	**USR**	C0	RET NZ	SET 0,B	
193	**STR$**	C1	POP BC	SET 0,C	
194	**CHR$**	C2	JP NZ,nn	SET 0,D	
195	**NOT**	C3	JP nn	SET 0,E	
196	**BIN**	C4	CALL NZ,nn	SET 0,H	
197	**OR**	C5	PUSH BC	SET 0,L	
198	**AND**	C6	ADD A,n	SET 0,(HL)	
199	<=	C7	RST 0	SET 0,A	
200	>=	C8	RET Z	SET 1,B	
201	<>	C9	RET	SET 1,C	
202	**LINE**	CA	JP Z,nn	SET 1,D	
203	**THEN**	CB		SET 1,E	
204	**TO**	CC	CALL Z, nn	SET 1,H	
205	**STEP**	CD	CALL nn	SET 1,L	
206	**DEF FN**	CE	ADC A,n	SET 1,(HL)	
207	**CAT**	CF	RST 8	SET 1,A	
208	**FORMAT**	D0	RET NC	SET 2,B	
209	**MOVE**	D1	POP DE	SET 2,C	
210	**ERASE**	D2	JP NC,nn	SET 2,D	
211	**OPEN #**	D3	OUT (n),A	SET 2,E	
212	**CLOSE #**	D4	CALL NC,nn	SET 2,H	
213	**MERGE**	D5	PUSH DE	SET 2,L	
214	**VERIFY**	D6	SUB n	SET 2,(HL)	
215	**BEEP**	D7	RST 16	SET 2,A	

Code	Character	Hex	Z80 Assembler	– after CB	– after ED
216	**CIRCLE**	D8	RET C	SET 3,B	
217	**INK**	D9	EXX	SET 3,C	
218	**PAPER**	DA	JP C,nn	SET 3,D	
219	**FLASH**	DB	IN A,(n)	SET 3,E	
220	**BRIGHT**	DC	CALL C,nn	SET 3,H	
221	**INVERSE**	DD	prefixes instructions using IX	SET 3,L	
222	**OVER**	DE	SBC A,n	SET 3,(HL)	
223	**OUT**	DF	RST 24	SET 3,A	
224	**LPRINT**	E0	RET PO	SET 4,B	
225	**LLIST**	E1	POP HL	SET 4,C	
226	**STOP**	E2	JP PO,nn	SET 4,D	
227	**READ**	E3	EX (SP),HL	SET 4,E	
228	**DATA**	E4	CALL PO,nn	SET 4,H	
229	**RESTORE**	E5	PUSH HL	SET 4,L	
230	**NEW**	E6	AND n	SET 4,(HL)	
231	**BORDER**	E7	RST 32	SET 4,A	
232	**CONTINUE**	E8	RET PE	SET 5,B	
233	**DIM**	E9	JP (HL)	SET 5,C	
234	**REM**	EA	JP PE,nn	SET 5,D	
235	**FOR**	EB	EX DE,HL	SET 5,E	
236	**GO TO**	EC	CALL PE,nn	SET 5,H	
237	**GO SUB**	ED		SET 5,L	
238	**INPUT**	EE	XOR n	SET 5,(HL)	
239	**LOAD**	EF	RST 40	SET 5,A	
240	**LIST**	F0	RET P	SET 6,B	
241	**LET**	F1	POP AF	SET 6,C	
242	**PAUSE**	F2	JP P,nn	SET 6,D	
243	**NEXT**	F3	DI	SET 6,E	
244	**POKE**	F4	CALL P,nn	SET 6,H	
245	**PRINT**	F5	PUSH AF	SET 6,L	
246	**PLOT**	F6	OR n	SET 6,(HL)	
247	**RUN**	F7	RST 48	SET 6,A	
248	**SAVE**	F8	RET M	SET 7,B	
249	**RANDOMIZE**	F9	LD SP,HL	SET 7,C	
250	**IF**	FA	JP M,nn	SET 7,D	
251	**CLS**	FB	EI	SET 7,E	
252	**DRAW**	FC	CALL M,nn	SET 7,H	
253	**CLEAR**	FD	prefixes instructions using IY	SET 7,L	
254	**RETURN**	FE	CP n	SET 7,(HL)	
255	**COPY**	FF	RST 56	SET 7,A	

The system variables – quick reference

The number in column 1 is the number of bytes in the variable. For two bytes, the first one is the less significant byte.

Bytes	Address	Sinclair Name	Contents
8	23552	KSTATE	Used in reading the keyboard.
1	23560	LAST K	Stores newly pressed key.
1	23561	REPDEL	Time (in 50ths of a second) that a key must be held down before it repeats. This starts off at 35, but you can **POKE** in other values.
1	23562	REPPER	Delay (in 50ths of a second) between successive repeats of a key held down: initially 5.
2	23563	DEFADD	Address of arguments of user-defined function if one is being evaluated; otherwise 0.
1	23565	K DATA	Stores 2nd byte of colour controls entered from keyboard.
2	23566	TVDATA	Stores bytes of colour, **AT** and **TAB** controls going to television.
38	23568	STRMS	Channel address attached to streams.
2	23606	CHARS	Pointer to the character set.
1	23608	RASP	Length of warning buzz.
1	23609	PIP	Length of keyboard click.
1	23610	ERR NR	Error report code (less 1).
1	23611	FLAGS	Basic flags.
1	23612	TV FLAG	Television flags.
2	23613	ERR SP	Error return address.
2	23615	LIST SP	Address of the automatic listing return address.
1	23617	MODE	Cursor type K, L, C, E or G.
2	23618	NEWPPC	Basic line to be jumped to.
1	23620	NSPPC	Basic statement number in line to be jumped to.
2	23621	PPC	Basic line number of statement currently being executed.
1	23623	SUBPPC	Number within a Basic line of statement being executed.
1	23624	BORDCR	Border colour * 8 and the attributes used for the lower half of the screen.
2	23625	E PPC	Number of current line (with program cursor).
2	23627	VARS	Basic variables address.
2	23629	DEST	Address of variable in assignment.
2	23631	CHANS	Channel data address.

Bytes	Address	Sinclair Name	Contents
2	23633	CURCHL	Address of information currently being used for input and output.
2	23635	PROG	Address of Basic program.
2	23637	NXTLIN	Address of next line in Basic program.
2	23639	DATADD	Address of terminator of last DATA item.
2	23641	E LINE	Address of command being typed in.
2	23643	K CUR	Address of cursor.
2	23645	CH ADD	Address of the next character to be interpreted.
2	23647	X PTR	Address of the character after the ? marker.
2	23649	WORKSP	Address of temporary work space.
2	23651	STKBOT	Address of bottom of calculator stack.
2	23653	STKEND	Address of start of spare space.
1	23655	BREG	Calculator's B register.
2	23656	MEM	Address of area used for calculator's memory.
1	23658	FLAGS2	Flags.
1	23659	DF SZ	The number of lines (including one blank line) in the lower part of the screen.
2	23660	S TOP	The number of the top program line in automatic listings.
2	23662	OLDPPC	Line number to which **CONTINUE** jumps.
1	23664	OSPCC	Number within line of statement to which **CONTINUE** jumps.
1	23665	FLAGX	Flags.
2	23666	STRLEN	Length of string type destination in assignment.
2	23670	SEED	The seed for **RND**. This is the variable that is set by **RANDOMIZE**.
3	23672	FRAMES	3 byte (least significant first). Frame counter. Incremented every 20ms.
2	23675	UDG	Address of 1st user-defined graphic.
1	23677	COORDS	x-coordinate of last point plotted.
1	23678		y-coordinate of last point plotted.
1	23679	P POSN	33-column number of printer position.
1	23680	PR CC	Less significant byte of address of next position for **LPRINT** to print at (in printer buffer).

Bytes	Address	Sinclair Name	Contents
1	23681		Not used.
2	23682	ECHO E	33-column number and 24-line number (in lower half) of end of input buffer.
2	23684	DF CC	Address in display file of **PRINT** position.
2	23686	DFCCL	Like DF CC for lower part of screen.
1	23688	S POSN	33-column number for **PRINT** position.
1	23689		24-line number for **PRINT** position.
2	23690	SPOSNL	Like S POSN for lower part.
1	23692	SCR CT	Scroll counter.
1	23693	ATTR P	Permanent current colours.
1	23694	MASK P	Used for transparent colours, etc.
1	23695	ATTR T	Temporary current colours.
1	23696	MASK T	Like MASK P, but temporary.
1	23697	P FLAG	Flags.
30	23698	MEMBOT	Calculator's memory area.
2	23728		Not used.
2	23730	RAMTOP	Address of last byte of Basic system area – RAM TOP.
2	23732	PRAMT	Address of last byte of physical RAM.

Hexadecimal conversion chart

Hex	Decimal	Binary
00	0	00000000
01	1	00000001
02	2	00000010
03	3	00000011
04	4	00000100
05	5	00000101
06	6	00000110
07	7	00000111
08	8	00001000
09	9	00001001
0A	10	00001010
0B	11	00001011
0C	12	00001100
0D	13	00001101
0E	14	00001110
0F	15	00001111
10	16	00010000
11	17	00010001
12	18	00010010
13	19	00010011
14	20	00010100
15	21	00010101
16	22	00010110
17	23	00010111
18	24	00011000
19	25	00011001
1A	26	00011010
1B	27	00011011
1C	28	00011100
1D	29	00011101
1E	30	00011110
1F	31	00011111
20	32	00100000
21	33	00100001
22	34	00100010
23	35	00100011
24	36	00100100
25	37	00100101
26	38	00100110
27	39	00100111
28	40	00101000

29	41	00101001
2A	42	00101010
2B	43	00101011
2C	44	00101100
2D	45	00101101
2E	46	00101110
2F	47	00101111
30	48	00110000
31	49	00110001
32	50	00110010
33	51	00110011
34	52	00110100
35	53	00110101
36	54	00110110
37	55	00110111
38	56	00111000
39	57	00111001
3A	58	00111010
3B	59	00111011
3C	60	00111100
3D	61	00111101
3E	62	00111110
3F	63	00111111
40	64	01000000
41	65	01000001
42	66	01000010
43	67	01000011
44	68	01000100
45	69	01000101
46	70	01000110
47	71	01000111
48	72	01001000
49	73	01001001
4A	74	01001010
4B	75	01001011
4C	76	01001100
4D	77	01001101
4E	78	01001110
4F	79	01001111
50	80	01010000
51	81	01010001
52	82	01010010
53	83	01010011
54	84	01010100

55	85	01010101
56	86	01010110
57	87	01010111
58	88	01011000
59	89	01011001
5A	90	01011010
5B	91	01011011
5C	92	01011100
5D	93	01011101
5F	94	01011110
5F	95	01011111
60	96	01100000
61	97	01100001
62	98	01100010
63	99	01100011
64	100	01100100
65	101	01100101
66	102	01100110
67	103	01100111
68	104	01101000
69	105	01101001
6A	106	01101010
6B	107	01101011
6C	108	01101100
6D	109	01101101
6E	110	01101110
6F	111	01101111
70	112	01110000
71	113	01110001
72	114	01110010
73	115	01110011
74	116	01110100
75	117	01110101
76	118	01110110
77	119	01110111
78	120	01111000
79	121	01111001
7A	122	01111010
7B	123	01111011
7C	124	01111100
7D	125	01111101
7E	126	01111110
7F	127	01111111
80	128	10000000

81	129	10000001
82	130	10000010
83	131	10000011
84	132	10000100
85	133	10000101
86	134	10000110
87	135	10000111
88	136	10001000
89	137	10001001
8A	138	10001010
8B	139	10001011
8C	140	10001100
8D	141	10001101
8E	142	10001110
8F	143	10001111
90	144	10010000
91	145	10010001
92	146	10010010
93	147	10010011
94	148	10010100
95	149	10010101
96	150	10010110
97	151	10010111
98	152	10011000
99	153	10011001
9A	154	10011010
9B	155	10011011
9D	156	10011100
9D	157	10011101
9E	158	10011110
9F	159	10011111
A0	160	10100000
A1	161	10100001
A2	162	10100010
A3	163	10100011
A4	164	10100100
A5	165	10100101
A6	166	10100110
A7	167	10100111
A8	166	10101000
A9	169	10101001
AA	170	10101010
AB	171	10101011
AC	172	10101100

Hex	Dec	Binary
AD	173	10101101
AE	174	10101110
AF	175	10101111
B0	176	10110000
B1	177	10110001
B2	178	10110010
B3	179	10110011
B4	180	10110100
B5	181	10110101
B6	182	10110110
B7	183	10110111
B8	184	10111000
B9	185	10111001
BA	186	10111010
BB	187	10111011
BC	188	10111100
BD	189	10111101
BE	190	10111110
BF	191	10111111
C0	192	11000000
C1	193	11000001
C2	194	11000010
C3	195	11000011
C4	196	11000100
C5	197	11000101
C6	198	11000110
C7	199	11000111
C8	200	11001000
C9	201	11001001
CA	202	11001010
CB	203	11001011
CC	204	11001100
CD	205	11001101
CE	206	11001110
CF	207	11001111
D0	208	11010000
D1	209	11010001
D2	210	11010010
D3	211	11010011
D4	212	11010100
D5	213	11010101
D6	214	11010110
D7	215	11010111
D8	216	11011000

Hex	Dec	Binary
D9	217	11011001
DA	218	11011010
DB	219	11011011
DC	220	11011100
DD	221	11011101
DE	222	11011110
DF	223	11011111
E0	224	11100000
E1	225	11100001
E2	226	11100010
E3	227	11100011
E4	228	11100100
E5	229	11100101
E6	230	11100110
E7	231	11100111
E8	232	11101000
E9	233	11101001
EA	234	11101010
EB	235	11101011
EC	236	11101100
ED	237	11101101
EE	238	11101110
EF	239	11101111
F0	240	11110000
F1	241	11110001
F2	242	11110010
F3	243	11110011
F4	244	11110100
F5	245	11110101
F6	246	11110110
F7	247	11110111
F8	248	11111000
F9	249	11111001
FA	250	11111010
FB	251	11111011
FC	252	11111100
FD	253	11111101
FE	254	11111110
FF	255	11111111

Hexadecimal conversion chart

	0	1	2	3	4	5	6	7	8	9	A	B	C	D	E	F
0	0	1	2	3	4	5	6	7	8	9	10	11	12	13	14	15
1	16	17	18	19	20	21	22	23	24	25	26	27	28	29	30	31
2	32	33	34	35	36	37	38	39	40	41	42	43	44	45	46	47
3	48	49	50	51	52	53	54	55	56	57	58	59	60	61	62	63
4	64	65	66	67	68	69	70	71	72	73	74	75	76	77	78	79
5	80	81	82	83	84	85	86	87	88	89	90	91	92	93	94	95
6	96	97	98	99	100	101	102	103	104	105	106	107	108	109	110	111
7	112	113	114	115	116	117	118	119	120	121	122	123	124	125	126	127
8	128	129	130	131	132	133	134	135	136	137	138	139	140	141	142	143
9	144	145	146	147	148	149	150	151	152	153	154	155	156	157	158	159
A	160	161	162	163	164	165	166	167	168	169	170	171	172	173	174	175
B	176	177	178	179	180	181	182	183	184	185	186	187	188	189	190	191
C	192	193	194	195	196	197	198	199	200	201	202	203	204	205	206	207
D	208	209	210	211	212	213	214	215	216	217	218	219	220	221	222	223
E	224	225	226	227	228	229	230	231	232	233	234	235	236	237	238	239
F	240	241	242	243	244	245	246	247	248	249	250	251	252	253	254	255

Memory map

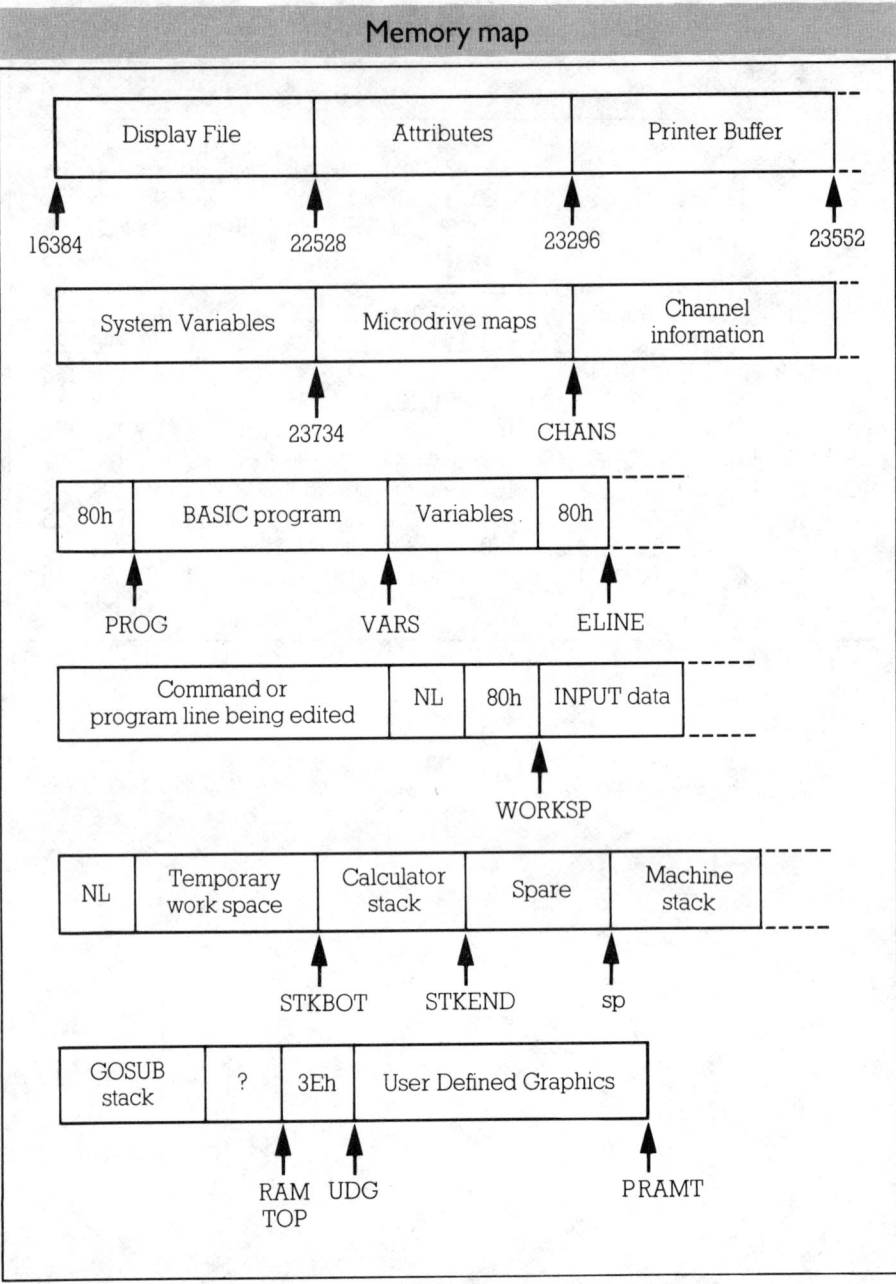

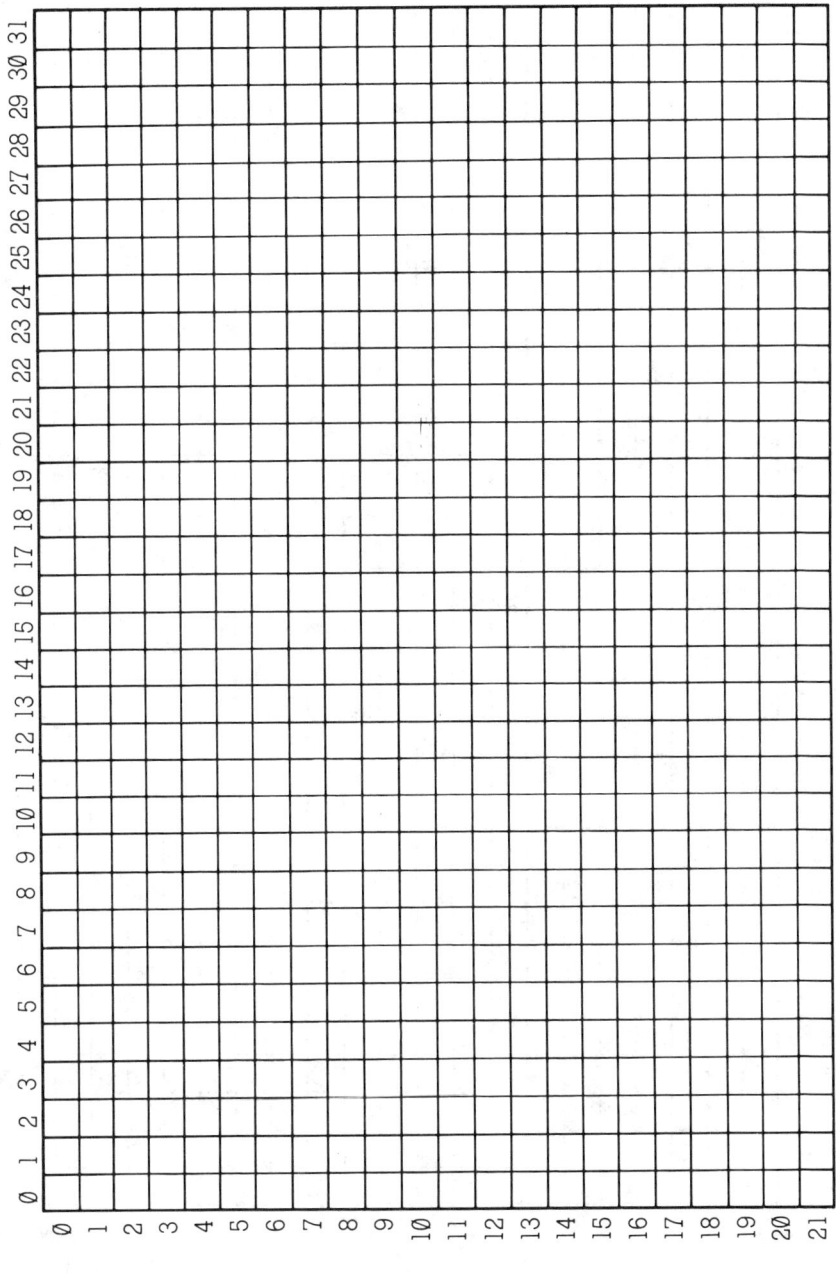

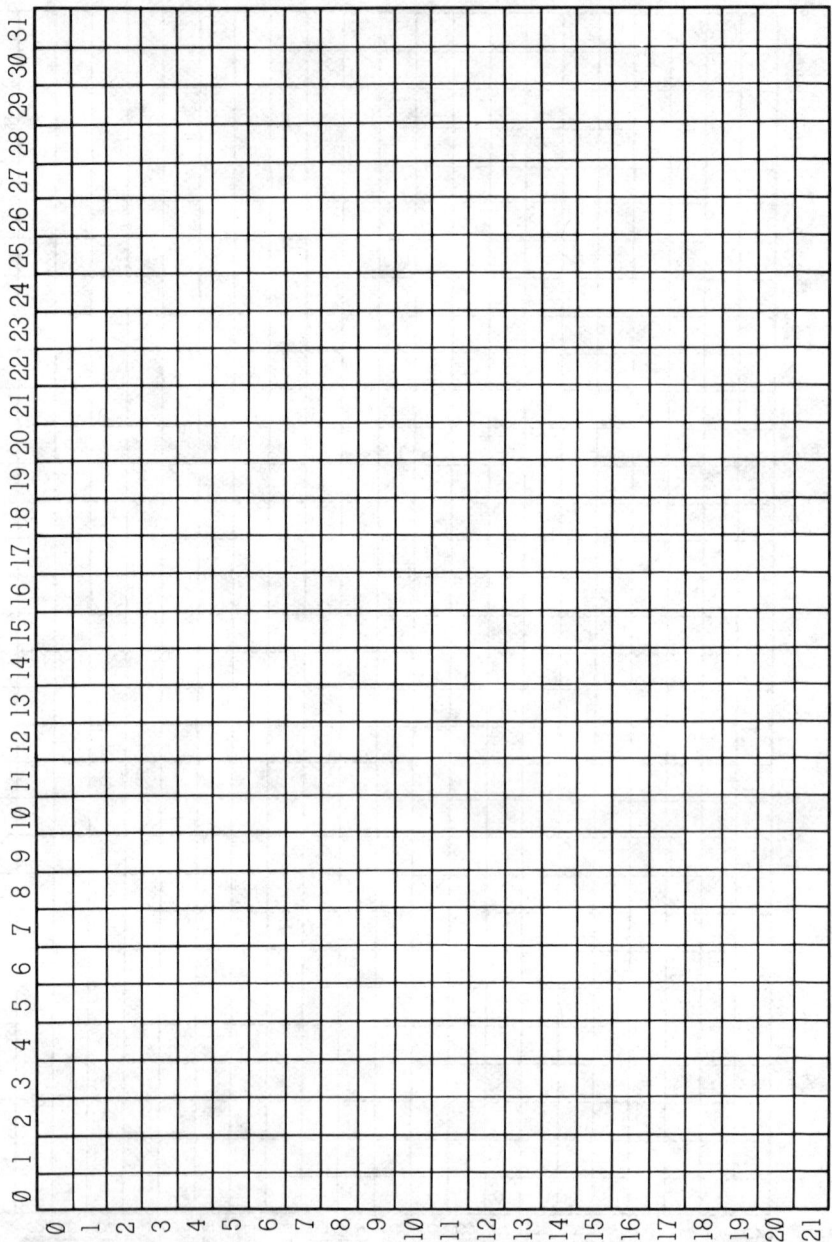

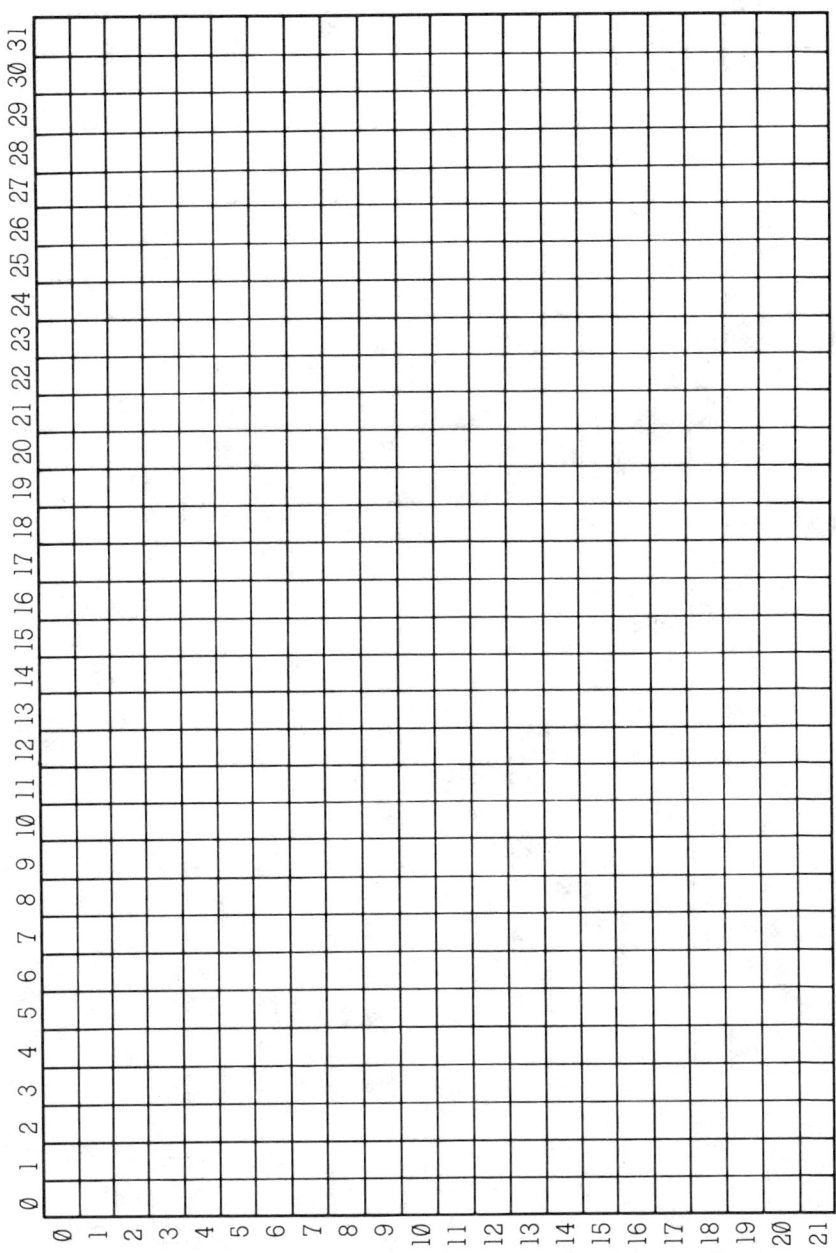

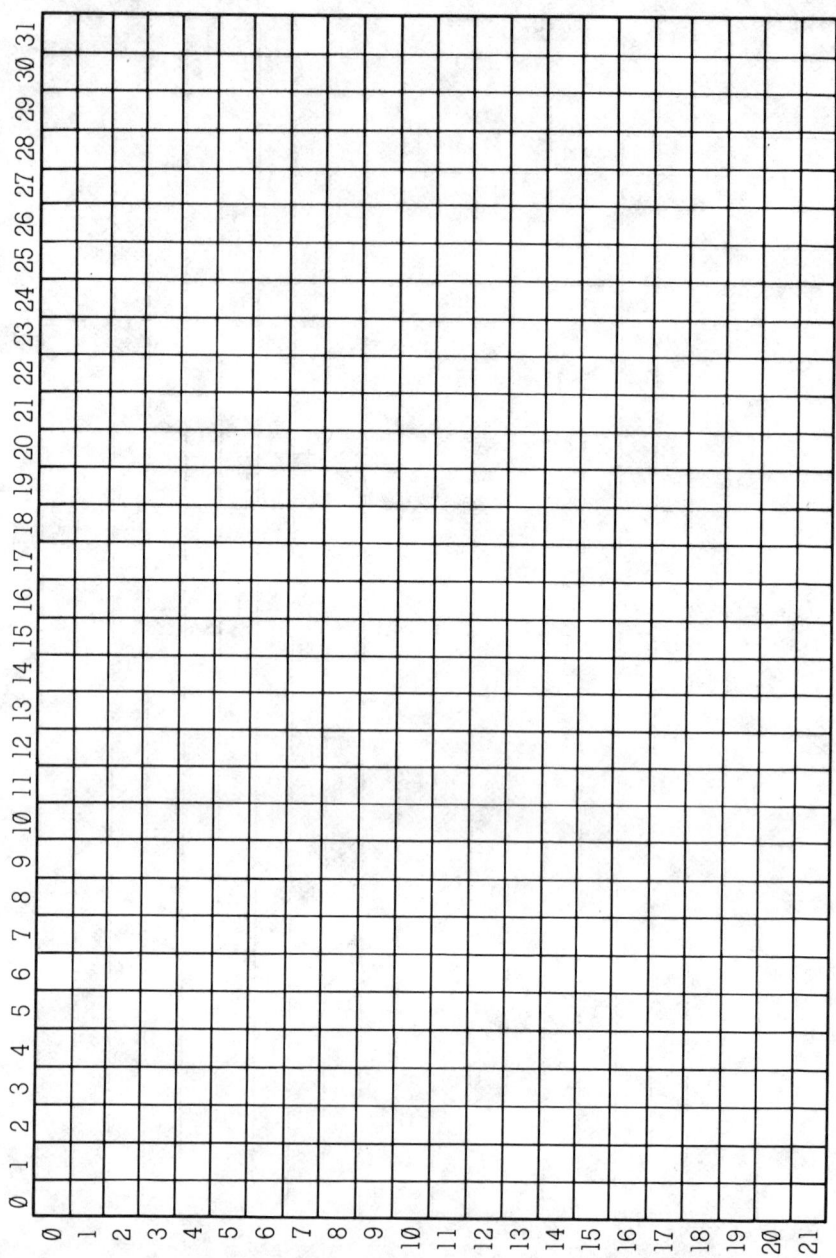

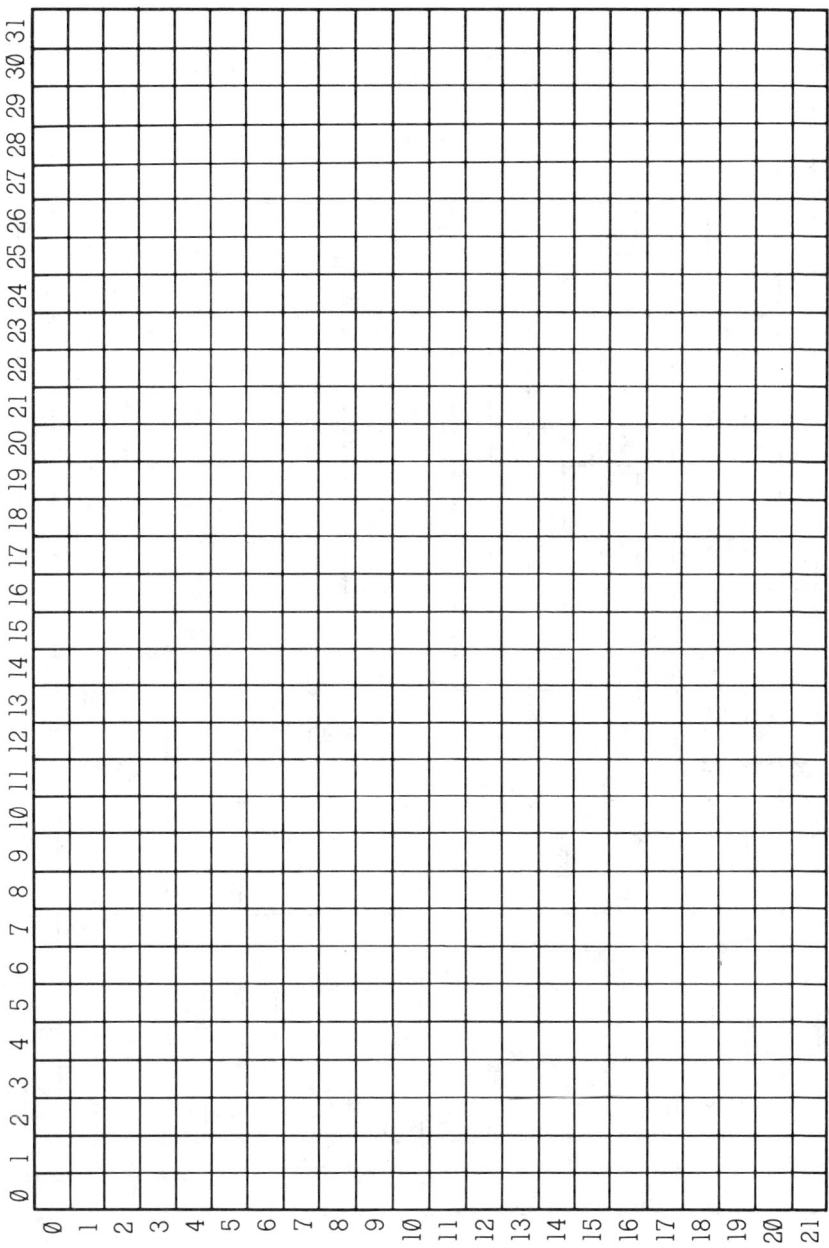

Appendix

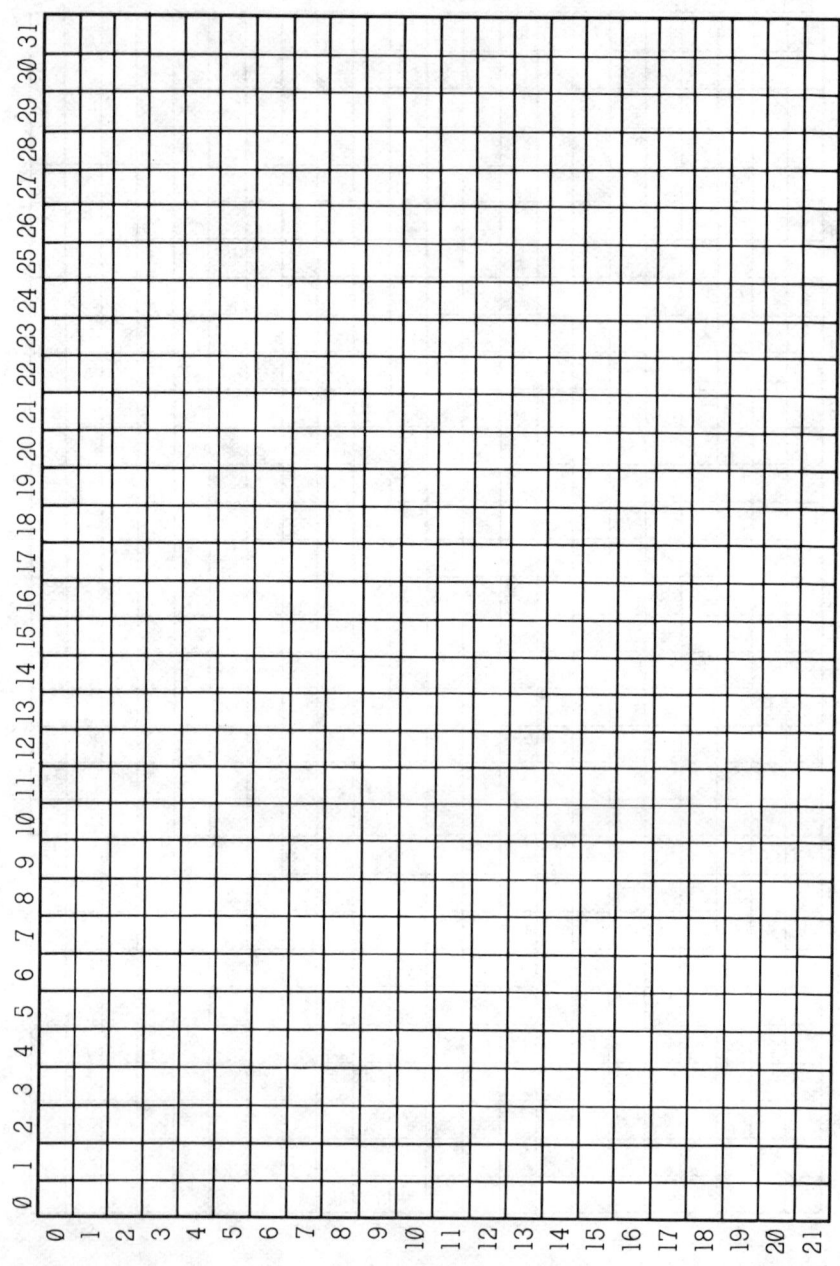

Appendix

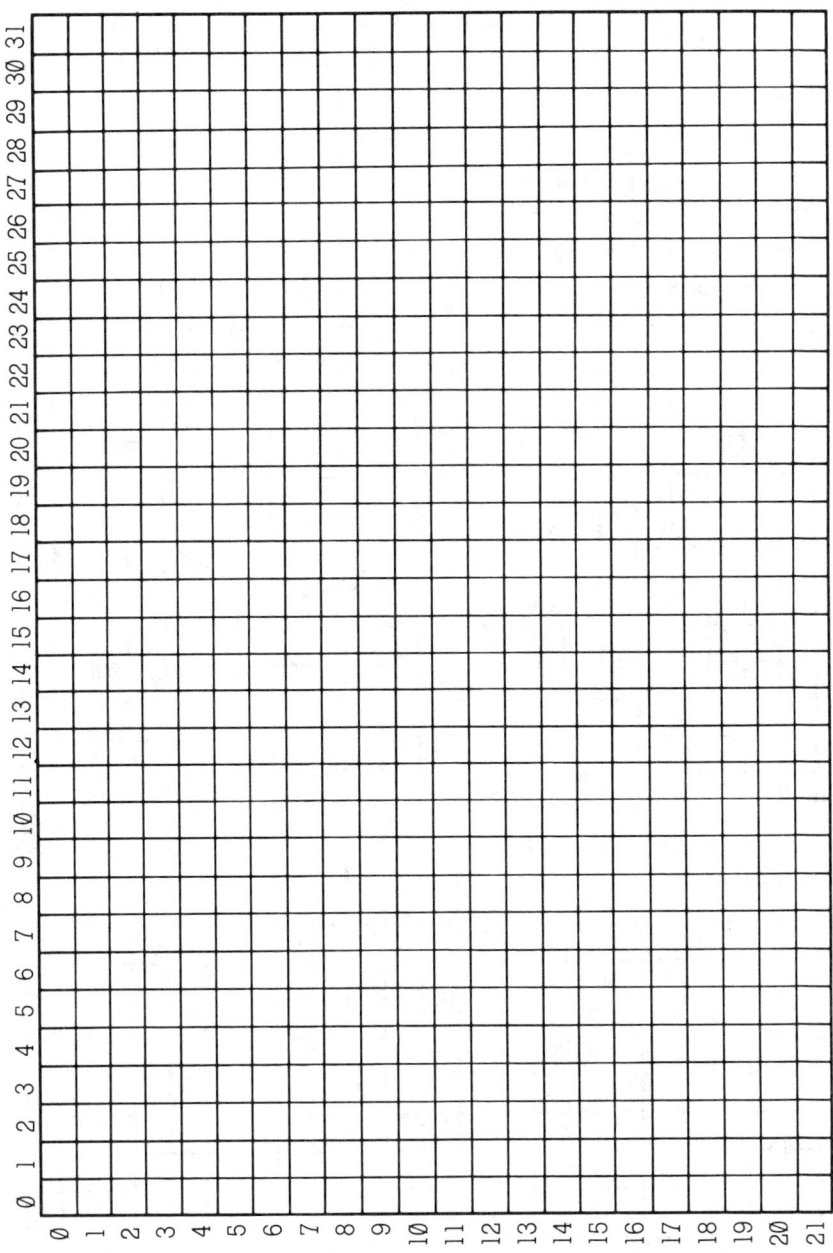

Appendix

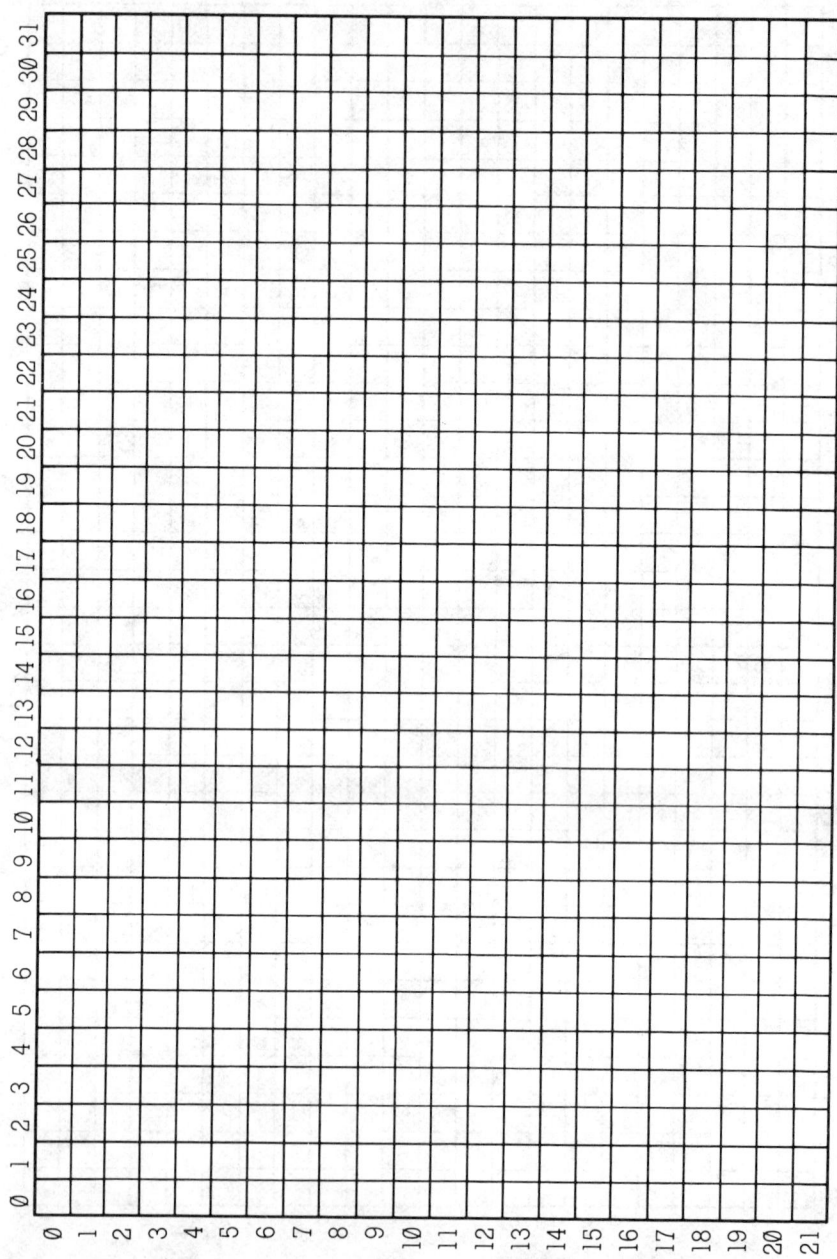

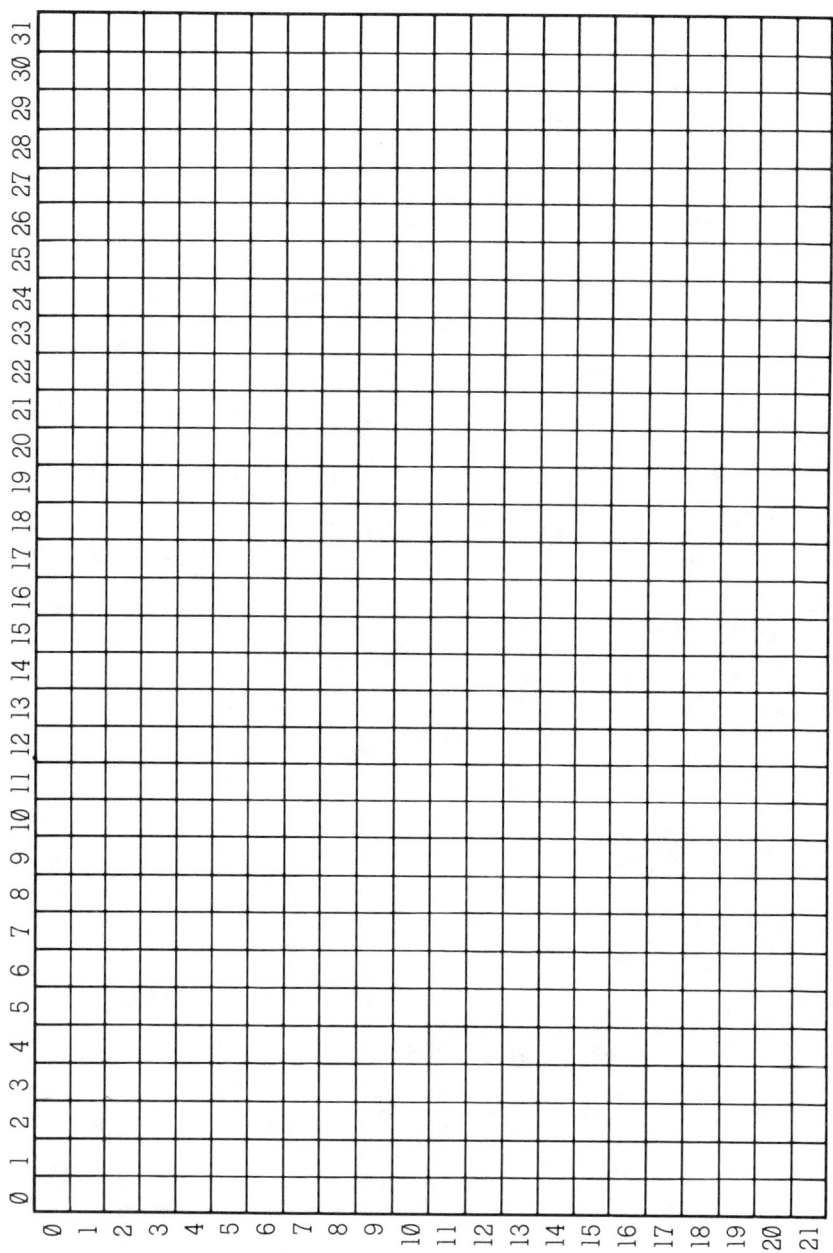

Index

A
ABS 20
ACS 21
address 60
adventure 42
AND 14
animation 90
arrays 33
ASCII 69
ASN 21
assembler 101
ATN 21
ATTR 87

B
Basic interpreter 100
BEEP 103
BIN 80
binary 80
branching 13
built-in functions 17

C
Centronics 119
channels 70
character positions 50
character set 70
CHARS 87
CHR$ 29
clock 76
CODE 27, 61
colour 57, 65
COS 21

D
DATA 32
DIM 33
display file 51
DRAW 50

F
field editor 37
flags 72
flats 108
FOR... NEXT 15

frequency 108
functions 18

G
GOSUB 8
GO TO 8
graphics 22, 49, 79
grassfibre fill 54

H
hexadecimal 101

I
information handling 32
INK 50
INKEY$ 27
INPUT 27
INT 20
interactive programming 25
Interface 1 118, 119
Interface 2 123
interrupts 102

L
LEN 27
local area network 120

M
machine code 101
memory 99
memory map 57, 103
MENU 35, 43
Microdrive 118

N
NOT 14
notes 108

O
octave 108
OR 14
output port 103

P
PAPER 50

PEEK 69
pixels 50
PLOT 50
pointer 83
pseudo random number 18

R
radians 21
RAMTOP 51
RANDOMIZE 19
RANDOMIZE USR? 101
READ 32
REM 43
RESTORE 33
RND 18
Rs232 119

S
scanning beam 91
screen 50
SCREEN$ 51
scroll 78
seed 18, 76
semitones 108
SGN 20
sharps 108
SIN 21
sound 101, 107
sprites 90
stack pointer 72
streams 70
string array 42
structure 8
subroutines 10
system variables 68

T
TAN 21
to fill 54

U
ULA 91
user-defined graphics 80
USR 53

V

VAL 27
vibrate 110
video RAM 91, 93